Politics and the Emergence of an Activist International Court of Justice

Politics and the Emergence of an Activist International Court of Justice

Thomas J. Bodie

Foreword by Don C. Piper

PRAEGER

Westport, Connecticut
London

Library of Congress Cataloging-in-Publication Data

Bodie, Thomas J.
    Politics and the emergence of an activist International Court of
Justice / Thomas J. Bodie : foreword by Don C. Piper.
       p. cm.
    Includes bibliographical references and index.
    ISBN 0–275–95014–X (alk. paper)
    1. International Court of Justice.   2. Political questions and
judicial power. I. Title.
JX1971.6.B62   1995
341.5′52—dc20   94–37739

British Library Cataloguing in Publication Data is available.

Library of Congress Catalog Card Number: 94–37739
ISBN: 0–275–95014–X

First published in 1995

Praeger Publishers, 88 Post Road West, Westport, CT 06881
An imprint of Greenwood Publishing Group, Inc.

Printed in the United States of America

The paper used in this book complies with the
Permanent Paper Standard issued by the National
Information Standards Organization (Z39.48–1984).

10 9 8 7 6 5 4 3 2 1

Copyright Acknowledgment

The author and publisher gratefully acknowledge permission to reprint
material from the following copyrighted source:

Excerpts from Brochard, Edwin M., "The Distinction Between Legal
and Political Questions," 18 ASIL Proc. 50 (1924). Reproduced with
permission from 82 ASIL Proc. 242 (1988), copyright © The American
Society of International Law.

For Sharon, Seth, and Caleb, for their sacrifices, patience, love, and support. Without them, nothing (including writing a book) would have meaning.

Contents

Foreword

According to conventional wisdom, the International Court of Justice, sitting in The Hague and consisting of 15 judges from different countries and legal systems and elected by a cumbersome process that involves both the United Nations General Assembly and the Security Council, is by the nature of things forced to play a very limited role in the settlement of international disputes. The tribunal, like any international tribunal, is not to be compared to a domestic tribunal, especially one like the U.S. Supreme Court. Rather, the Court is expected to play a limited and focused role that is restricted to the careful interpretation of clearly defined and agreed upon rules of international law. Such a limited role is necessary because of the limitations and imperfections in the international legal system itself, the absence of any effective enforcement mechanism to ensure compliance with the Court's rulings, and the lack of consensus among the states of the international community regarding what issues are to be considered "legal" and therefore potentially resolvable by third-party measures and what issues must be considered "political" and therefore not susceptible to judicial settlement.

Those who study international law and the activities of the International Court of Justice continually confront the frequent and persistent fallacies of conventional wisdom regarding the strengths and weaknesses of international law. In this instant work, Thomas J. Bodie dispels some of the fallacies of conventional wisdom about the inadequacies and limitations of the International Court of Justice. Bodie demonstrates that, since its inception in 1920 as the Permanent Court of International Justice under the League of Nations, the World Court has progressively moved away from a narrow, legalist interpretation of its role to become an activist tribunal. Over time the Court has moved beyond a narrow focus on exclusively "legal" issues and has adopted a more encompassing view of itself as one of the organs of the United Nations system that is to play a particular and useful role in dispute settlement. In this role the Court is prepared to take under its purview disputes that involve significant political aspects, including questions regarding a state's employment of armed force. This does not mean that the Court has abandoned legal issues and has become a political body. Rather, the Court has become more willing to consider and pronounce upon facts and respective legal rights that are enmeshed in controversial and ongoing political disputes between states.

As the Court continues to move in this new direction, it will likely offend some states and please others. The outrage expressed by the Reagan administration with the Court's acceptance of the case brought against the United States by Nicaragua and the subsequent statement by the Legal Adviser announcing the U.S. withdrawal from the optional clause of the Court's Statute reflect a view that challenges the Court's activist approach. It is not clear at the present time how far the Court is prepared to go, or will be able to go without causing a significant number of states to follow the United States and withdraw from the optional clause, in pursuing its activist role. At the same time, it is difficult to comprehend the Court retreating from its activist approach. The Court will, no doubt, attempt to achieve a balance such that it remains an activist tribunal without losing its jurisprudential credibility or legitimacy.

Thomas J. Bodie's work gives us the foundation to confront conventional wisdom about the Court but also, and more importantly, it enables us to appreciate the dynamic and creative forces operating in the international legal system that enable the Court in particular and the rules of international law in general to assume a more visible and important role in the conduct of international relations. These same dynamic forces also make the study of international relations so important and so exciting. We are indebted to him for his contribution to the field of study.

Don C. Piper
University of Maryland

Acknowledgments

I thank all the professors at the University of Maryland, College Park, with whom I interacted. On some level, each and every one of them is somewhere in this.

I owe my greatest debt to my advisor, Professor Don C. Piper, for all his ideas, assistance, friendship, and what must have been incredible forbearance in the face of my incessant worrying. He would have every right to get an unlisted phone number after this experience. But for some reason, he keeps on providing me with a support system—thanks.

I also thank Professors Richard P. Claude, Earllean McCarrick, Larman Wilson, and David Segal, for serving on my committee. Their time and efforts on my behalf are greatly appreciated. I also extend my gratitude to James R. Ice, Liz Murphy, Dina K. Rubin, and Kathleen Taylor at the Greenwood Publishing Group, for all their work on shepherding this project through to completion. By now, probably no one's time and effort on this manuscript has exceeded that of Sharon Furman—it's a shame that this herculean word-processing chore had to come at the expense of her sanity.

I would finally like to thank my wife, Sharon A. Sykora. It takes plenty of patience to put up with me in normal times. It took all the patience of the gods to put up with me while writing this. Her editing and suggestions made this work better. Her love makes me better.

Introduction

On April 9, 1984, the Republic of Nicaragua filed an application with the International Court of Justice instituting proceedings against the United States of America. Nicaragua sought legal relief from what it claimed were unlawful acts of aggression, in the forms of military and paramilitary activities, carried out by the United States against the Republic of Nicaragua. In its counter-memorial, the United States attempted to press the claim that the case did not fall within the jurisdiction of the Court. Several arguments were presented by the United States. First, the questions presented by Nicaragua showed textually demonstrable commitment to another international organ. In other words, this was a peace and security issue of the type charged to the *political* organs of the U.N. (i.e., the Security Council), not the *legal* organ. Second, there was no judicially discoverable and manageable standard on the basis of which the legal obligations of the parties could be adjudged. In other words, armed conflict is too amorphous for the abilities of a judicial body. Third, the situation was already the subject of negotiations under the umbrella of the Contadora process. Therefore, the Court should not interfere where political processes were already at work. In short, the United States asserted that the dispute "is an inherently political problem that is not appropriate for judicial resolution." The Court found otherwise.[1]

Nicaragua v. the United States of America (hereinafter referred to as *Nicaragua*) is only one battle in a very long war, a war over the jurisdictional boundaries of international tribunals, maybe even the very boundaries of international law itself. At issue is the following question: Is there subject matter in international discourse over which international law does not rule? In other words, *may international relations be divided into legal and non-legal realms*? If this question has a positive answer, then there exists an arena in which states may act unilaterally, unbeholden to any higher authority such as the law, unencumbered by the restraints of third parties with ajudicatory power. The modern history of international tribunals, including ad hoc arbitration panels, the Permanent Court of Arbitration set up by The Hague Conventions of 1899 and 1907, the Permanent Court of International Justice (PCIJ) created by the League of Nations, and the International Court of Justice (ICJ) created with the United Nations, has been plagued with this debate. Examining how these bodies dealt with the jurisdictional questions inherent in cases before them will add to the conclusions reached by the end of this book.

The special focus of this book shall be on this jurisdictional problem, examining the distinction that has been drawn between *legal* and non-legal, or *political*, issues. I will investigate the history of this debate, in the theoretical work of scholars, in the words of international agreements, and in the practical work of various international tribunals.

There are certain definitional questions that should be dealt with at this point, regarding the words *jurisdiction* and *justiciability*. Jurisdiction is the widest of these terms, defined by *Black's Law Dictionary* as "the power of the court to decide a matter in controversy and presupposes the existence of a duly constituted court with control over the subject matter and the parties." Justiciable is defined by *Black's* as that which "refers to a real and substantial controversy which is appropriate for judicial determination."

One aspect of this jurisdictional debate has suggested that there are some issues which, by their very nature, are non-justiciable. The solution to such problems cannot be found through the law. Rather, these problems must be solved through the give and take methods of the political process. In short, some issues are legal, some are political, and these two categories are distinguishable. (Greater definition of this distinction will be found in the words of scholars and courts, contained throughout the rest of the book.) Through document analysis, case study, and doctrinal examination, this book means to discover whether or not such a political question doctrine exists in international law.

What will be seen by the end of this work is that in international law, justiciable has been something of a nebulous term, having meaning only as states give it meaning. In other words, states have attempted unilaterally to decide what is appropriate for judicial determination. The result is that the meaning of justiciable has fluctuated from state to state, from issue to issue, and across time. As this research will also show, however, the ICJ has had its own thoughts in determining what is appropriate. And, as a result of the International Court of Justice's actions, justiciable may need redefining. That will be taken up in Chapter 5.

(Immediately, attention should be drawn to a possible terminology problem that could arise for any reader familiar with U.S. constitutional law. In U.S. constitutional law, there is a political question doctrine that attends to relations between the various branches of the government. When international law specialists discuss political questions, they are referring to a jurisdictional question that must be answered by international tribunals arbitrating or adjudicating a dispute between states. No one should confuse these two different uses of the term "political question." This book is concerned strictly with what the term signifies for international law.)

Is there a need for research on this subject? Ian Brownlie has written that "the writer who takes up the problems of the justiciability of disputes has some duty to explain why it is thought that there is anything to be said which adds to the substance of Hersch Lauterpacht's book *The Function of Law in the International Community* which was published in 1933."[2] In fact, Lauterpacht's work *was* seminal. But it is the most important statement for only one side of the justiciability debate—a debate that has not yet ended.

There is a need for an investigation such as this. First, and foremost, there has never been any final answer given regarding the possible division between legal and political questions. Those who have written on this subject have not agreed about whether the doctrine should even exist at all. This should be clear just from the above brief discussion. Fresh attempt is therefore still worthwhile.

Historical context must also be taken into account when determining the need for this effort. The changing nature of international relations throughout this century has been reflected in the scholarly literature. For example, a change seems to have occurred within the body of literature on this subject around the time of World War II. Before the war, examinations of compulsory jurisdiction (Lauterpacht is one example) tended to be legalistic in nature, the assumption being that the boundaries between legal and political (if any were to be found at all) could be brought to light solely on the basis of legal reasoning. This would seem to reflect the idealism (if not actual state practice) inherent in the creation of the League of Nations. Any issue could be settled by resort to law.

After the war, even this small measure of idealism was all but gone. The boundary between legal and political was assumed, and was couched in power politics. The question is not what *should* be expected, but rather, what *could* be expected in a cold-war world. The realists held forth now—either the issues were too complex for the simplicity of adjudication, or the reality of national security interests could not be overcome.

Beyond this, the researcher who undertakes this subject is cautioned by some that not only does a division between legal and political disputes exist, but it is impossible to draw any set lines marking the boundaries of these two areas. Edward McWhinney approvingly quotes Hermann Mosler on this, and suggests that the reason for this "impossibility" is that, given the ever-changing nature of international law, "the frontiers of justiciability/non-justiciability may be constantly shifting or changing."[3]

But now the historical context is changing again. For one thing, ideological tension is lessening worldwide. The demise of the Soviet Bloc and the end of the cold war have increased the opportunities for use of the Court. The old

Soviet position was that a court populated mostly by justices from capitalist states, applying capitalist legal doctrines, could not be trusted to be evenhanded vis-á-vis socialist states.   That position was undergoing change even under Mikhail Gorbachev, with the Soviets announcing that they were prepared to make use of the Court.   Now that the Soviet Union has broken up into its component republics, there is even greater possibility of such increased use.

The increasing utilization of the International Court of Justice stretches beyond just the events in Eastern Europe of the last few years. The Court recently has received a great increase in applications submitted to it, many of which involve states that have never previously appeared before the Court. Currently, the Court has the fullest docket it has ever had. With all of this activity, there will likely arise questions over justiciability. Certainly, the *Nicaragua* case should indicate that the debate over justiciability is still alive.   Simply put, reexamination of this debate is timely, given all this new activity.

Chapter 1 shall be an analysis of the writings of other scholars on this subject. This is not a simple literature review. Normally, literature reviews are more cursory undertakings placed within the first chapter of a book and are meant to show how the present work differs from works that have preceeded it. For the international law work, however, a more detailed examination is required. This is so because, for international law, the writings of publicists and scholars are taken as secondary evidence of the law. Therefore, these writings serve not only as scholarly research, but also as the current interpretations of what the law actually is.

The volume of work to be examined will be large. This distinction between legal and political issues was first raised by Vattel in 1758. It took life as a serious issue in the latter half of the nineteenth century, as arbitration gained favor as a method of dispute resolution between states.   It then became important to know which issues were appropriate in nature for such tribunals to hear. The import of all this for the present purpose is that there exists a great deal of scholarly input on the subject, some of which is significant in the treatment of the issue and some of which is simply descriptive. Some selection of representative pieces is therefore required.

What the reader will discover is that there are far more representative pieces from the realist school than from the idealists. This should not be seen as bias on the part of the author; rather, it is simply indicative of the state of the discipline. Among scholars in the field, realism, and its inherent conclusion that there are limits to juridical power in the international arena, is the theoretical position chosen most often. As the reader will find out, this no longer defines the position of the International Court of Justice. The importance of Chapter 1 lies in its showing how wide the chasm between the opinion of the Court and that of the scholars has become. In other words, the preponderance of realism among the scholarly community only serves to highlight the position of the Court, which, I posit, is idealist.

In Chapter 2, a review will be conducted of this justiciability debate as it has played itself out in the processes of international arbitration. There will be two lines of examination. Down one line, a review of arbitration treaties will be conducted. This will take account of such multilateral general conventions as The Hague Conventions of 1899 and 1907 and the General Treaty of 1928. Additionally, there are several hundred bilateral treaties in existence that call for disputes over the subject matter of the treaty to be resolved by arbitration. Some of these treaties are considered archetypes after which other treaties have been modeled. The majority of these arbitration treaties contain some sort of reference to legal versus non-legal disputes, making inclusion of them important here.

The other line of examination in Chapter 2 will be a search for this legal/political dichotomy in the actual decisions of arbitration tribunals. From the *Alabama* arbitration of 1872 forward, arbitration tribunals, or the states creating the rules under which the tribunals work, have had to struggle with this issue.

What should come of this examination is a sense of state practice regarding the differentiation between legal and non-legal in international law. As will be seen, states have been very consistent in drawing the distinction. As with Chapter 1, this conclusion will serve to highlight the different opinion the ICJ has of the matter.

Chapter 3 will undertake an examination of the Permanent Court of International Justice. Created by the League of Nations in the wake of World War I, both the Court's Statute and the decisions rendered will have import here. As a result, this chapter's survey will be patterned after the two-track approach of Chapter 2—a document analysis plus a review of actual decisions. Much debate over justiciability went into the creation of the Statute of the Court. Recognition from the justices of this debate over the breadth of their jurisdiction is also evident in the decisions of the Court.

Chapter 4 will repeat the process of Chapters 2 and 3, only in this instance, it will be for the International Court of Justice, created as part of the United Nations in 1945. Again, evidence from the Court's Statute that shed's light on this topic will be included. And, the decisions of the Court will be analyzed for evidence of what the justices of the ICJ have thought about this justiciability issue.

Chapter 5 will bring together the results of Chapters 1, 2, 3, and 4, attempting to find similarities or differences in opinion over the entire course of this debate. Are there governing paradigms? Have these changed at all over the last century? Charting scholarly opinion should be easy, given the work of Chapter 1. State practice will be gleaned from Chapters 2, 3, and 4. After all, appearance before international tribunals is a voluntary act by states. Discerning which issues states have allowed before third parties and which have been withheld produces evidence of states' opinion on the justiciability of disputes.

This may also be seen in the governing Statutes of the PCIJ and the ICJ, and in the arbitration treaties and conventions, as these were all created by the states themselves.

It is also important to have the input of those individuals who have been granted the power to make the jurisdiction decisions in the actual cases—the justices and the arbitrators of the various international tribunals. In any case brought before any court, before reaching the merits of the case, the question of competence must first be answered. So it is with an international court. This justiciability debate has recurred again and again. What these tribunals have defined as their own boundaries should be very important contributions to this discussion.

Does all this evidence point to one clear-cut answer to the problem? Or does disagreement reign, producing only confusion? How does this speak to the very definition of the term justiciable? Sythesizing all of the collected evidence will be the goal of Chapter 5.

Finally, I will draw some conclusions regarding the current status of this legal/political dichotomy in international law. As indicated previously, the questions here are: "Does this dichotomy exist?" and "Should this dichotomy exist?" Based on the conclusions I reach regarding these questions, I will make my own recommendations regarding the changes I see as necessary for international law.

Previous Inquiries

The enormous task of tracing scholarly work in a field of study as old as international law might at first give one reason to pause. Thankfully for this author, however, the distinction between legal and political issues in international law received little treatment prior to the latter half of the nineteenth century. It is about that time that states began to challenge one another in international tribunals, introducing into debate the question of which issues it could appropriately be said were subjects of third-party judgments, a debate willingly taken up by interested scholars and lawyers.

Even limiting one's examination to the latter half of the nineteenth century forward, however, is no small task. It requires some framework for manageably following the evolution of scholarly thought on the subject. One possibility is to view it on a time line. Interestingly enough, that time line may be broken up into three sections, these sections divided by the two world wars of the twentieth century: pre-World War I, interwar, and post-World War II.

The first differentiation between legal and non-legal issues in international law actually was made by Emmerich de Vattel in 1758, when he distinguished between two different types of rights. He does take positive note of arbitration, writing: "Arbitration is a very reasonable means, and one that is entirely in accord with the natural law, of terminating every dispute which does not directly affect the safety of the State."[1] But then he immediately issues a caveat that states are not to entrust their survival to arbitral tribunals. There are two very different types of disputes in relations between states: "In the disputes which arise between sovereigns, a careful distinction must be made between essential rights and less important rights, and a different line of conduct is to be pursued accordingly."[2]

Pursuing different lines of conduct meant for Vattel that "essential rights" were not justiciable and "rights of lesser importance" were justiciable. Until the end of World War I, this distinction between interests and rights, political and legal, was the prevailing view. State practice confirmed this, as reflected in many of the treaties of the nineteenth and early twentieth centuries.

This identification of legal versus political issues by the states was simultaneously upheld as theoretically correct by international law scholars. The subject was taken up again (in the same condition Vattel left it) when actual events in the latter half of the nineteenth century precipitated further discussion. The increased utilization of arbitration led to the need for more careful definition by legal scholars over just which issues were succeptable to arbitration, hence legal.

That a distinction could be drawn was a given. The scholarly community was nearly unanimous in its opinion that some issues could be decided by third parties and some could not, and most were convinced that the former category was much smaller than the latter. The argument from all of the writers of this period may come forth in different words, but the main theses are generally fashioned in the same way.

One way to draw the distinction was simply to compare a dispute against some nebulous "code" of international law. If there were rules in existence that provided guidance to the resolution of the dispute, then it was a legal issue. If there were no rules, or the rules that did exist were ambiguous, then it was a non-justiciable issue. Hence, Oppenheim wrote:

> International differences can arise from a variety of grounds. They are generally divided into legal and political. Legal differences are those in which the parties to the dispute base their respective claims and contentions on grounds recognized by International Law. All other controversies are usually referred to as political or as conflicts of interests.[3]

John Westlake also provides a very good example of this argument in favor of drawing the distinction. Westlake wrote of legal questions: "By a legal difference between states, one is meant which can be settled by reference to known rules, having at their back that force which is derived from the general consent of the international society."[4]

Westlake fleshed out this standard with several examples. In the cases he raised, the issues that were of legal content included treatment of a foreign national, claims of sovereignty on the high seas, and an arbitration where the rules to be applied to the case are expressly agreed upon in advance by the contending parties.

As far as Westlake was concerned, "political action is justifiable", and thus rules of international law are non-existent or no longer applicable or relevant, in three cases. One such case arises when no rule that fits the particular circumstance has been agreed upon by the international community. A second instance is when a rule has become outdated. For lack of some international governing body to overturn the law, it must simply be broken at some point. The third case is when applicable rules are imperfect or imprecise, leaving wide room for interpretation.

As his example, Westlake points to the Treaty of Paris of 1856, by which France and Great Britain constricted Russia's military use of the Black Sea. Limitations placed upon a state on what it may do within its own territory will be temporary rulemaking, lasting only so long as a particular power configuration lasts. Once Russia determined that France was no longer in a position to enforce the treaty, Westlake allowed that that meant Russia could break it.

The problem with this example of a political issue is that it does not fit any of the three categories that Westlake listed for political disputes. Westlake attempted to propose a very law-like sounding standard by which one could differentiate between legal and political disputes. In practice, he could not avoid power considerations in judging that difference. The breaking of this treaty was strictly a balance of power calculation, devoid of any reference to international laws. And if Westlake is apt to allow national security considerations into the debate of legal verus political, how much more so will states? This points up the larger problem with Westlake's standard—it is too general. It relies on the interpreter. Westlake had his list of "known" rules. But, given the evolutionary nature of international law, and differing scholarly and diplomatic opinion on what has become "generally accepted" at any particular point in time, there are bound to be many different opinions on what is "known" to be a rule of international law.

Another defense of the distinction between legal and political was much more unabashedly national security-oriented. This argument, more often seen among international law scholars, simply declared that there were naturally two different spheres of activities at the international level. Some issues were political not merely because international law did not reach them, but rather because law had nothing to do with them.

This argument normally carries with it national security implications. Certain events, decisions, or interactions between states may or may not have implications for the future security of the states involved. But only those states can make that judgment. A sense of security is a subjective thing. There are no standards for saying just how secure "secure enough" is. Every state must make that decision for itself. Outsiders cannot make those decisions. This holds true whether by "outsiders" one means those who would enforce international law, or one means international law itself. Therefore, there is a realm of activities that lies outside international law. That realm is called politics.

For example, Thomas Balch was the instigator of the resort to arbitration in the *Alabama* case, by way of an 1865 letter to the *New York Tribune*. In that letter, Balch's opinion was that the American and British claims were "such as to rest upon questions of law."[5] As such, they were arbitrable. These claims could be distinguished from those that were "strictly national" in nature. Presumably, these national issues were not arbitrable. When he wrote "that as to such claims [legal], war was a barbarous manner of enforcing them," Balch drew further distinction between legal and political issues—legal issues are those not important enough to bring about war.

British scholar James Lorimer wrote to Balch in 1874 with regard to his letter to the *Tribune*, which was now to be published as part of a book. Commenting on the subject matter, Lorimer also drew a sharp distinction between legal and political issues, recognizing that one of "the chief difficulties attending international arbitration" was "the character of the questions that can be submitted to them."[6] Fleshing out what was meant by character, Lorimer wrote: "Arbitration is inapplicable where the question at issue has reference to the relative value of States—where it is asked, for example, whether their historical position in relation to each other is or is not now their true position."[7]

For an example of historical position, Lorimer referred to the Franco-German war. The technical causes of the war were boundary disputes, and to Lorimer, these would have been suitable for arbitration. However, insofar as that war "was a fight for the hegemony of continental Europe, it did not admit of arbitration."[8] Great power status, according to Lorimer, could only be settled by a test of strength: war.

There is a form of the national security argument that goes even further in favor of the individual state. This argument, too, recognizes both legal and political disputes. But for proponents of this position, even when the law is clear and applicable to the dispute at hand, states are allowed to ignore it. Thus, Thomas Willing Balch writes:

> The expression, *legal cases*, should be recognized to mean questions arising between nations which while a cause of dispute between two or more sovereign states, *do not* threaten by their solution in favor of one side or the other, the independence or any vital interest of either party. The expression, legal cases, furthermore, should be recognized to apply to all those cases which do not affect the vital interests of the contesting nations, whether there are or are not rules of the law of nations upon which the majority of the great powers of the world are agreed, ready at hand to apply to such cases in arriving at a judicial decision for their solution.
>
> The expression, *political cases*, should be recognized to mean questions arising between states which, owing to the facts and interests involved in those cases, do threaten, in any attempt to solve those questions by a judicial decision, in the future to affect and alter either favorably or unfavorably the political power and influence of

one or more of the nations parties to the controversy. The expression, political cases, furthermore, should be recognized to apply to all those cases which do affect the vital interests of the contending nations; even though there may be rules of international law generally recognized by the nations the application of which to those cases would decide them strictly on legal grounds in favor of one side or the other.[9]

For Balch, even where the rules exist, a state may find it odious to follow those rules. If a state makes a judgment that some international law impinges on its security, as that state defines its security, then by Balch's definition that dispute becomes political. This position would strip international law of any pretense it would have of being law. International law becomes totally consensual in all instances.

That a distinction could be drawn between legal and political disputes in international relations was the governing paradigm until World War I. By the war's end, that paradigm was broken. Something was clearly wrong with a system that could lead to such a devastating event as this war. What was necessary were systemic changes. If institutional settings were created that would allow states to pursue peaceful conflict resolution, then maybe this last war truly could be "the war to end all wars." The years following the war were a heady time in international relations. A new world order was being created. Nations were supposed to be submitting their disputes to the League of Nations and the Permanent Court of International Justice. In such an atmosphere, it is easy to see how some legal scholars could view the distinction between political and legal issues as one of the problems with the old system. Such a distinction had allowed states to throw a cloak of legitimacy around their politics-as-usual pursuit of self-defined security interests. The vigorous debate of this period allowed some scholars the opportunity to argue that all disputes could and should be settled by third-party means. Certainly, this new position did not just simply replace the old paradigm—proponents of drawing a distinction did not just go away. But this new position, that nothing was non-justiciable, became an important addition to the discussion.

The work of Edwin Borchard is representative of this idealist position. In his portion of a report on the issue for the American Society of International Law, Borchard questions whether such a distinction really existed for any reason more than the convenience of states. On this he deserves extensive quotation:

Is not the criterion of legal or justiciable or arbitrable questions other than that commonly suggested? Does it not lie less in the fundamental nature of the question than in the willingness of the nation to submit it to judicial determination; in the importance which the question is deemed to possess for the national interests rather than in its source?

In other words, without disputing the usefulness of the description of legal questions frequently presented, is the distinction not a subjective rather than an objective one? If the question does not affect what the nation may deem to be its vital interests, or if it finds that it has less to lose by a judicial settlement than by war or other political method, it will be submitted and will by many for that reason be called legal. Were not the political issues involved in the *Alabama* and Venezuelan questions submitted to arbitration because Great Britain deemed that mode of settlement preferable to political hostilities with the United States? Thus, what is known as a political question becomes a legal question solely because there is a willingness, induced by any one of many considerations counselling self-restraint, to have it peaceably settled. Certainly the absence of a pre-existing or known applicable rule of law can be no deterrent to such settlement, for courts have from their earliest days made the law for the case when they found no existing applicable rule. This is recognized as a normal judicial function and exemplifies the precise method by which the common law was developed. No case has ever been dismissed or rejected because there was no pre-exising rule of law to apply to the case.

On the other hand, the most legal of questions, such as the interpretation of a treaty, may not be submitted to judicial settlement because it involves an issue important to the nation's so-called vital interests, deemed vital perhaps by itself alone. It may prefer to rely upon the arbitrament of war rather than submit it to the determination of third parties, though all the lawyers in the world will call it a legal question.[10]

Borchard refers in the above passage to the "usefulness of the description of legal questions." At first this may seem contradictory to his overall position. But while he takes pains to label this classification "harmful" and "inaccurate," Borchard concedes that such a distinction might serve in the short run to focus the attention of the concerned public. If a set of issues were set aside as arbitrable or adjudicable, states might, perhaps, be reminded that "certain types of questions can and should be settled by peaceful or judicial methods."[11] In other words, if the distinction is going to be maintained by states, false as that distinction may be, then at least the discussion should then revolve around how to make it a distinction providing a service. Nevertheless, Borchard's main argument remains—no logical distinction really does exist between legal and non-legal issues.

In the same report, Manley O. Hudson sets out to illustrate "the impossibility of drawing any sharp lines between legal and political questions" through an account of the Corfu crisis between Italy and Greece.[12] As Hudson puts it, while there were political aspects to the case, the same could be said of most contentious cases, international or municipal. The role of law is to settle these cases, regardless of political underpinnings. In fact, according to Hudson, this is the process by which law advances. Therefore, it does not make sense to attempt to segregate any class of disputes as non-justiciable. Hudson's prominence as a scholar and justice of the Permanent Court made his voice fairly influential.

The most in-depth examination of the position that there was no separate category for political disputes belongs to Sir Hersch Lauterpacht. Lauterpacht expounds on this very subject, the distinction between legal and political, in his book, *The Function of Law in the International Community*. He begins the book by tracing for the reader the origins of the doctrine of non-justiciability. It is, as he describes it, a direct result of the doctrine of sovereignty. This latter doctrine results in states reserving for themselves, "first, as the right of the State to determine what shall be for the future the content of international law by which it will be bound; secondly, as the right to determine what is the content of existing international law in a given case."[13]

With the rise of international arbitration, lawyers and scholars had to overcome fears of the loss of sovereignty in order to convince states to utilize third-party settlement processes. This was done by narrowing the definition of what was susceptable to those processes and what would still be the strict domain of the states—what was justiciable and what was non-justiciable.

For Lauterpacht, believing as he does that no disputes are non-justiciable, the next step is to refute each of the reasons generally given for drawing a distinction between legal and political issues. The first argument to come under his gaze is that which asserts that legal issues are only those in which a judge or a panel may find the existence of rules of international law applicable to the settlement of the dispute, a phrasing of the problem not unlike Westlake's formulation. This position is easily disposed of by Lauterpacht. International law is not unlike municipal law, he says, in that it is a system of law governing a community. Municipal law, too, has its gaps. Situations may arise that municipal codes do not speak to directly. And yet judges are expected, even required, to hand down a decision in every instance. The rule of law is complete. As such,

> it is impossible, as a matter of *a priori* assumption, to conceive that it is the will of the law that its rule should break down as the result of the refusal to pronounce upon claims. There may be gaps in a statute or in the statutory law as a whole; there may be gaps in the various manifestations of customary law. There are no gaps in the legal system taken as a whole.[14]

It is the same, he argues, with international law. It is not necessary to have, and might even be ludicrous to expect, a code that speaks to every dispute. But judges can still hand down just decisions. Rather, a legal system's existence is more rightly based on the willingness of its subjects "to submit their disputes to a final decision of the judge."[15] Therefore, that international law may appear incomplete is no reason to *a priori* limit its purview.

The next argument to which Lauterpacht turns his attention is the contention that political issues are those that affect the vital interests of a state—what I have earlier referred to as the national security argument. This argument is based on the distinction first drawn by Vattel that there are minor and major issues in which states become involved. Major issues are deemed too important for states to cede sovereignty to a third party. This proposition inevitably leads to the question, "Which issues fall into which categories?" An ordering of issues is required. Most often, this takes place on an *ad hoc* basis. A dispute arises, and then a state decides whether it is important. I believe such decision making will tend, more often than not, to place the dispute in the category of a political dispute, given the passions of the moment. This may suggest that even timing is important in a state's determination of legal versus political. Immediacy exaggerates the importance of a dispute. Thus, whereas prior to the Argentine invasion of the Falklands there had been suggestions in British circles of placing the Falklands' future in the hands of third-party resolution, after the invasion the perceived threat to the honor of Great Britain made a legal solution impossible at that time, as far as the British were concerned.

But as Lauterpacht points out, even where attempts have been made in the past to create comprehensive lists of what is justiciable and what is not, ahead of time in a general convention, issues are seen more often than not as *possibly becoming* important. Thus, as the German delegate to the 1907 Hague Convention noted, even a matter as technical as the use of railway cars might become political in time of war.

To Lauterpacht, this debate over the categorization of issues is misguided. All issues are at once both political and legal. All disputes are political by virtue of the fact that they involve states: "The state is a political institution, and all questions which affect it as a whole, in particular in its relations with other States, are therefore political. As such they are deemed to be important."[16] And any dispute may be seen in only its political context if that is how a state is predisposed to see it.

But this state of affairs does not mean that there are international disputes that are incapable of legal resolution. To Lauterpacht, "so long as the rule of law is recognized, they are capable of an answer by the application of legal rules." Lauterpacht presents a host of examples of so-called political disputes, which he then examines for their legal aspects. Therefore, for him, there is no difference between disputes due to their importance. The difference only stems from the willingness of the states involved to recognize the legal aspects of a dispute and settle it as such.

The third argument in favor of a distinction between legal and political issues that Lauterpacht attempts to refute harkens back to the second of Westlake's three cases in which political action is justifiable. Westlake felt that the lack of a governing body in the international arena meant that some laws could not change apace with the needs of the international community. The result would be outdated laws for states to follow. As Lauterpacht notes, proponents of this argument also worry that this means there would be outdated laws for international tribunals to apply to disputes. In such an instance, there is the very likely opportunity for injustice to occur. Under these circumstances, states are more likely to forego adjudication so as to protect perceived "new" rights from "old" rules.

Lauterpacht lays out three main counterarguments to this position. In the first place, he argues, a great deal of the concern in the 1920s and 1930s over the rapid change of conditions in international relations stemmed in large part from "the changes in the territorial and other provisions imposed by force in recent peace treaties."[17] When states are forced to make concessions, it should come as no surprise that when power relations change, so will adherence to unjust treaty obligations. Normally, change of this sort is not the norm, and therefore it should not be held up as a real claim against judicial resolution of disputes.

Secondly, Lauterpacht notes that this position overemphasizes the possible benefits of legislated change. Why would it necessarily be the case that a majoritarian decision in a political body would be more apt to leave certain parties to a dispute feeling less aggrieved? If politics played too great a role in such a resolution, and those politics were simply reflective of the power relations in the dispute, why would the "losing" party not feel even more aggrieved? In such an instance, the aggrieved party might be even more inclined toward using force, not less. A decision that was viewed by the disputants as being based on rules of law might very well appear more fair than one based on politics.

And finally, adherents to this position underestimate the ability of the judiciary to adapt the law to changing conditions. Admittedly, a legislature is the traditional place for rule changes to occur, and one would not encourage the judiciary to usurp the legislature's powers. On the other hand, "these limitations do not materially alter the fact that courts do not slavishly administer abstract rules without being able to exercise creative discretion."[18] In other words, the courts would certainly be cognizant of the effect outdated rules would have on the dispensing of justice, and would move to resolve disputes in a just manner.

Closely connected to this third argument in favor of drawing a distinction between legal and political is the final class of so-called non-justiciable disputes Lauterpacht attends to, disputes in which the claimant does not profess to have the law on its side. In fact, the claimant might even go so far as to acknowledge that it is "legally in the wrong."[19] These claims are not for existing rights, but for supposed new rights. They are claims based solely on interests. Examples he provides include claims on another state's territory, not out of a right to it, but due to an interest in it; or preventing the union of two states, not because they do not have the legal right to unite, but because the claimant state feels threatened by the proposal. But Lauterpacht treats this argument as nothing more than a slightly different form of the gaps-in-the-law argument discussed above. Courts are competent to decide their own jurisdiction, and to decide on the merits by reference to general principles of law.

The general argument put forward by Lauterpacht through all of these exercises of refutation is that while international law is in a relatively youthful stage, the problems it faces are theoretically the same as those faced by any system of law governing any political entity. The only truly unique problem it faces is the absence of compulsory jurisdiction over its subjects.

For Hans Kelsen, too, the way to peace was through adjudication. In fact, as far as he was concerned, one of the great flaws of the League of Nations system was that it set the political/administrative bodies, rather than the Permanent Court, at its center. Kelsen also believed with Lauterpacht that there was nothing inherent in any dispute that would label it a legal or political issue.

On numerous occasions Kelsen took up the question of legal and political conflicts. His position rested on drawing a distinction between the "nature of the dispute" and the "nature of the norms to be applied in the settlement of the dispute."[20] The nature of the dispute is the "subject matter to which the dispute refers,"[21] and always has economic or political characteristics. That does not mean, however, that the conflict may not be settled through legal means. As he notes in a frequently cited example:

> If A claims an estate which is in the possession of B and B refuses to comply with A's claim, the dispute is economic in nature; but to say that this dispute is not legal *because* it is economic is obviously absurd. It makes no difference that A and B are States and that the dispute concerns, instead of an estate, a part of the territory of B.[22]

There is nothing inherent in the subject matter of a dispute that defines it as legal or political. This differentiation is made through the settlement process. A dispute is legal if resolution is made through appeal to the norms of positive law (existing law); it is political if appeal is made to other standards such as justice or equity. Even at that, a tribunal applying such non-legal standards creates a decision that "constitutes an individual legal norm, the parties to the dispute being legally obliged to comply with it."[23] Which processes are utilized depends on the parties involved, of course, and that is where the subjectivity of the distinction lies. But, Kelsen holds, all disputes are capable of legal resolution.

The theoretical position of the idealist is that human nature is, for the most part, morally good. Humankind's bad behavior can be altered positively through the intervention of morally correct institutions. As noted above, this was the hope that underlay the creation of the League of Nations at the end of

World War I. Balance of power politics had failed—collective security would bring peace. It did not. The institutional apparatus of the League was unable to check the territorial and imperial aspirations of certain states, allowing the next paradigm-changing event, World War II.

Idealism/legalism still had its proponents after World War II. But the predominant theoretical position became that of realism. The best summary of this theory came forth in the work of Hans Morgenthau, most especially in his book, *Politics Among Nations*. Morgenthau contrasts realism with idealism; whereas the idealist believes in "abstract principles" and attempts to reeducate people to be better, the realist sees the world and its inhabitants for what they really are, and formulates policies that will "work with those forces, not against them." People are self-interested. Everyone having their own interests, the world is one "of opposing interests and of conflict among them." States are just larger expressions of this principle, and the overriding interest for a state is its security.

The relevant point for the present purposes is that sometimes a state's security and international law may be in conflict. The realist is cognizant of the importance of international law in some issue areas, and is even appreciative to a point. After all, it is in every state's interest that international intercourse be predictable. Rules create predictability and lessen the chance for conflict in a great many areas such as economic trade, diplomatic exchange, movement of people across borders, and the like. Having said that, however, the realist would suggest that law has its limits in the international arena. Remembering that states can be the only judges of their own interest, it can be seen that in some instances, states will not be able to surrender their decision-making processes to a third party such as an adjudicative body. The realist definitely sees a difference between legal and political issues.

Morgenthau divides conflictual events into three categories: pure disputes, disputes with the substance of a tension, and disputes representing a tension (he defines tensions as "unformulated conflicts of power"). What distinguishes these three categories one from another is whether there is simply an interpretation of existing law required, or if there is a desire (tainted by a power struggle) for a change in the status quo.

"Pure disputes" are disputes with no relationship to any other tensions. Two states may have a model relationship and still have a conflict over some issue. Two states may have adversarial relations, and still may have a conflict over some issue that has no relationship to any other tensions at all. The key is that these would most likely be minor, technical disputes. Monetary exchange rates for diplomats is Morgenthau's example. This type of dispute is the type that Morgenthau writes of being "susceptible to judicial decision." "Disputes with the substance of a tension" are directly connected to the power struggle. For example, Morgenthau suggests that any interpretation of the Potsdam Agreement would have impinged on the capabilities of the Soviet Union or the United States to pursue hegemony over Europe. Neither state could have allowed a third party to give forth a decision in such an instance. "Disputes representing a tension" are disputes that are imbued with symbolic value by the nations involved. As Morgenthau points out, this type of dispute could readily start as a pure dispute, but at some point, in the eyes of the contestants, the dispute comes to typify the very essence of the larger struggle and is seized upon and made "the concrete issue by which to test their respective strength."[24]

Pure disputes may be formulated in legal terms and may be separated from any underlying tensions (if there are any). As such, these disputes are susceptible of judicial decision. The other two types of disputes are not. They are part and parcel of the power struggle between the disputants. The idealist might be tempted to reformulate such a dispute in order to highlight those aspects that are capable of legal resolution. The realist would suggest that this is wrongheaded; that while adjudication might dispose of a dispute, it might not necessarily solve it. Lissitzyn wrote, "Even in the best organized states, many conflicts of interest cannot be terminated by judicial proceedings."[25] The realist declares that "to view such disputes solely from a legal perspective is to see but one facet of a multifaceted phenomenon."[26] Richard Falk wrote:

> Many international disputes that could be expressed in relation to legal rights and duties involve underlying conflicts about political control; the essence of the dispute involves a struggle that could go forward by military or non-military means. As such, disputes about legal rights and duties are epiphenomenal and their authoritative resolution will not eliminate the struggle.[27]

In other words, most disputes are far more complex than just the legal issues involved.

Ibrahim Wani urges the exercise of discretion by the Court for the benefit of husbanding the Court's authority. This position sounds much like Alexander Bickel's[28] position on the political question doctrine as applied domestically in the United States. (The reader is again reminded that there is no connection or analogy between this U.S. constitutional issue and political questions under examination here.) According to Bickel, the job of the judicial branch is to educate the people about the great principles that guide the republic. The courts must exercise discretion, however, picking just the right moment to elucidate such principles. In other words, on some occasions the timing is not right. The courts must pick their fights carefully, lest they look bad in the public's eyes. Those holding this position recognize that the courts have no real power to enforce their decisions. They cannot afford to have a decision ignored, or they would lose the moral strength they carry.

For some, it is the same argument at the international level. Martin Rogoff, raising these same concerns with regard to the ICJ, refers to international adjudication as "a fragile institution," and calls on the Court to "be sensitive to its institutional position."[29] As Wani writes:

> The most compelling argument for an international political question doctrine is based on prudential considerations. To paraphrase Justice Felix Franfurter, the International Court of Justice, lacking either the power of the purse or of the sword, needs to choose its battles carefully in order to maintain its integrity. The political question doctrine can be handy in avoiding politically controversial disputes and those that cannot be effectively resolved. This is not because there is anything inherently political about the disputes but rather simply as an expression of the Court's sense of its practical limitations.[30]

Wani recognizes state practice, and believes that states will ignore the World Court if too great an interest is at stake. Lissitzyn saw an inverse relationship involved when he observed, "The greater the interest at stake, the less likelihood there is of a contestant foregoing the advantages of a political settlement in which the power factor would work in his favor."[31]

It should be noted that there is no conflict between recognizing this problem *and* believing that there are no disputes that could arise that are inherently non-justiciable. This seems to be the position of both Wani and Hermann Mosler. The difference between these two in assigning responsibility for solving the dilemma is representative of the realists. Wani, as was just indicated, assigns responsibility to the Court. Mosler notes that the Court may not decline a dispute where there is jurisdiction. He lays the responsibility at the feet of the states themselves to use the Court wisely.[32]

It should be cautioned that holding the realist position does not mean one is arrayed against the Court. R. P. Anand spends quite a bit of time justifying many of the realists' positions, especially the position that as long as states refuse to see the legal angles of their disputes, and continue to accept only negotiated (read power-influenced) resolutions, they will not look upon legal decisions as "solving" the underlying factors of conflicts. He even quotes Oliver Wendell Holmes to the effect that "the life of the law has not been logic; it has been experience."[33] Having said all this, however, Anand goes on to call the Court a "powerful constituent element of peace", and urges that "it is essential to increase the jurisdiction of the courts."[34]

The truth of the matter is that realism all but chased idealism from academia. While idealism of the Lauterpacht/Kelsen variety did not simply vanish in the aftermath of World War II, there were few left who regarded all disputes as justiciable. One heir to the mantle is Rosalyn Higgins.

Higgins examines the legal/political dichotomy as expressed through the differences of opinion between British and American lawyers over the role of international law and the rules of legal interpretation. She is squarely in favor of the more policy-oriented approach of the American lawyers, and disposes of each of the arguments in favor of drawing distinctions between legal and political disputes. There cannot be "non-legal" disputes, to be thought of as political and "social, humanitarian and moral issues,"[35] since bringing about desirable social outcomes is, after all, the whole underlying *rasion d'etre* of the law. She concludes that: "the terms 'political dispute' and 'legal dispute' refer to the decision-making process which is to be employed in respect of them, and not in the nature of the dispute itself."[36]

Almost as if she were taking her cue straight from Borchard, it is clear that she lays the blame at the feet of the states themselves, for these distinctions are really the result of their subjectiveness. Then, like Lauterpacht and Kelsen, she does not satisfy herself with accepting that states should be allowed to continue the charade. The situation should not be allowed to continue simply because it has "realistically" been that way—institutional changes are in order. Thus, she writes: "If it is felt that courts are ill equipped to deal with policy matters, and if policy matters are indeed an unavoidable part of the legal process, then the only rational alternative is to improve the capabilities of the courts in this respect."[37]

Higgins represents a tiny minority, however. Realism was such an overwhelming presence that even scholars advocating world government could not escape drawing a distinction between legal and political issues. Thus, Grenville Clark and Louis B. Sohn[38] called on states to surrender large chunks of their sovereignty to a new and greatly empowered United Nations. They advocated compulsory jurisdiction for third-party conflict resolution. But they separated disputes to be resolved into those of a legal nature and those of a non-legal nature, each type to be heard by a different panel. Even as strong an advocate of international law as Louis Henkin[39] sees limitations for the law, and criticizes those who do not see such limits.

There have been, over the years, various strains of thought on this law/politics dichotomy. There are those who have maintained that no such distinction exists, that all disputes are justiciable. However, this group of scholars is greatly outnumbered by those who have asserted that a distinction between legal and political issues does exist. Certainly, it appears that this latter position is the current governing paradigm.

2

International Arbitration: The States in Action

Through a historical overview of selected arbitration treaties and arbitral decisions, I hope to find evidence of state practice in distinguishing legal from non-legal questions. This is because arbitration is a purely voluntary interaction between two or more states. Therefore, issues that states have been willing to arbitrate before an impartial tribunal should be, by definition, those issues that states view as justiciable.

This latter observation requires an immediate caveat, however. Nothing of a universal nature may be concluded from the ensuing presentation. Not every state has participated in arbitration, and certainly it is possible that states have changed positions over time on what is arbitrable. This latter event is especially possible given the lengthy time line utilized in this chapter.

On the other hand, it is clear that patterns have emerged over the years. Certain topics have consistently been arbitrated over time. Certain key phrases in treaties have gained acceptance or fallen out of favor. As the arbitration process became more commonplace, its subject matter was generally expanded by all. For example, most of the arbitrations that occurred during the nineteenth century happened as a result of an *ad hoc* decision-making process, each case being treated as a separate entity. Into the twentieth century, it was more commonplace to have general arbitration treaties that placed whole classes of disputes in the arbitrable category. All of this suggests that reaching some concrete conclusions will be possible.

There are many possible paths to dispute resolution provided for in the intercourse between states. Arbitration and adjudication stand apart from other techniques such as negotiation, mediation, and conciliation by virtue of the fact that there is a final judicial decision and the disputants are expected to execute the final decision of the tribunal. In other words, the decision of the tribunal is to be considered legally binding. Arbitration is to be distinguished from adjudication by the nature of the tribunal itself—while arbitrators are freely chosen for the case at hand by the disputants, this is not the case in adjudication, where there is a sitting court to hear cases. Arbitrators may be the head of a third state, any other neutral person or persons (including arbitrators of the Permanent Court of Arbitration), or a mixed commission composed of one or two nationals for each of the disputants plus a neutral umpire. Arbitrations may be entered into via a *compromis* (a special treaty concluded solely for settling the dispute at hand), general arbitration treaties calling for the process in certain classes of disputes, or compromissory clauses in non-arbitration treaties. The arbitrators are expected to respect the rule of international law in the final decision, unless the parties stipulate that the decision is to be based on some other agreed upon set of rules or on general principles of equity. And, as mentioned above, states must agree in advance both to accept and to carry out the final decision of the tribunal. The only exception to this last rule is in the rare instance of a tribunal handing down a decision clearly in excess of the jurisdiction originally extended to it by the parties. In this case, the decision becomes null and void.

Arbitration is a form of dispute resolution that has a history dating back to antiquity. Ralston provides a good summary of the arbitrations of ancient Greece. The majority appear to have been conducted between cities in the same league at the behest of the league's controlling power. But there were quite a few conducted between different leagues, thus raising them to a level we would today define as international arbitration. Additionally, Ralston indicates that compromissory clauses in treaties, providing for arbitration of disputes arising under the treaty, were frequent. For instance, the treaty between Sparta and Argos of 418 B.C. contained the following provision:

> If there should arise a difference between any of the towns of the Peloponnesus or beyond, either as to frontiers or any other object, there shall be an arbitration. If among the allied towns they are not able to come to an agreement, the dispute will be brought before a neutral town chosen by common agreement.[1]

Ralston is thorough in his history lesson, including the Roman attitude toward arbitration, several arbitrations between ancient peoples not Greek or Roman, and the use made of the procedure through the Middle Ages. But all of this activity predates the "modern" era of the nation-state system. For most scholars, modern arbitration begins with the Jay Treaty of 1794. It is in this treaty that we find the first attempt between nation-states to settle their differences by arbitration.

The Jay Treaty, so named by Americans after the American diplomat John Jay, was signed on November 19, 1794, between the United States and Great Britain. Three different arbitral boards were created by the treaty: one to settle a boundary dispute on the northern edge of the United States; a second to settle the private pecuniary claims of British citizens against the United States; and a third to settle American citizens' claims against Great Britain "by reason of irregular or illegal captures or condemnations of the vessels and other property, under color of authority or commissions from His Majesty." This commission also had jurisdiction over similar maritime claims by British citizens against the United States.

Several important precedents were established by the commissions of the Jay Treaty, including the power of a commission to determine its own jurisdiction, and the necessity of exhausting other judicial remedies (and also when it was not necessary) in order for disputes to go to the international level.[2] But probably the most lasting achievement of the Jay Treaty was to identify for statesmen of the time the usefulness of arbitration in settling disputes.

From this beginning, arbitration became a tool increasingly utilized by states. This was especially so for the United States and Great Britain. The United States and Great Britain utilized it again under the aegis of the Treaty of Ghent of December 24, 1814, to settle the outstanding disputes over the boundary between the United States and Canada. These two states again signed conventions on February 8, 1853, and July 1, 1863, submitting outstanding pecuniary claims to arbitration.

The most ground-breaking of all the arbitrations of the 1800s also took place between the United States and Great Britain, this being the arbitration to settle the historic *Alabama* claims. These cases arose out of U.S. claims against Great Britain for alleged violations of the obligations of neutrality during the conduct of the U.S. Civil War. The United States charged that Great Britain had allowed ships of the Confederacy (e.g., the *Alabama*) to be refitted into warships in its ports, in violation of the laws of neutrality. After the war, the United States made claims against Great Britain for damages caused by the *Alabama* and several other ships. Tense negotiations ensued, with both nations finally agreeing to submit the case to arbitration.

That arbitration was finally agreed upon was no small feat. In fact, it was probably the most significant aspect of the whole case. Both states had avoided the arbitration route initially on the grounds that national honor was at stake. For the British, the problem appears to have hinged on defending their "own long-cherished interpretation of the law of the sea."[3] In other words, for the British, it was an issue of pride—a traditional sea power being judged by outsiders over claimed violations of the law of the sea. For the United States, the great excitation of the general population at the end of the Civil War placed political pressure on the U.S. government. Due to the costs of the war, there was apparently great indignation over the appearance of interference by Great Britain in the cause of the Confederacy. It was this popular resentment that made negotiating a Court of Arbitration so difficult.[4]

The agreement to submit to arbitration was finalized through the Treaty of

Washington of May 8, 1871. The treaty itself actually "solved" the case, because it set up the rules under which the arbitrators were to work, known as the Three Rules of Washington. These rules actually laid out the responsibilities of a neutral state, demanding more of the neutral state than would have been the case under the law of nations in 1862. And clearly, under these three rules, Great Britain was in the wrong. All that was left for the arbitrators was to fix the amount of the award due the United States.

That more of the case was settled by the treaty than by the arbitrators does not detract from what took place. The negotiation of the treaty occurred pursuant to setting up the rules for an arbitration that had already been agreed to. What was significant about the settlement of these claims was that "national honor" was at stake as far as both states were concerned. Two large states had agreed to submit to arbitration a case that had brought them to the brink of a war. Until this point, arbitrations had been sporadic and had been over non-vital interests, settling disputes over such issues as boundaries, fisheries, maritime prizes, and pecuniary claims. This case really did serve to change the tone of international arbitration.

The United States concluded many other arbitration agreements with Great Britain during the 1800s. The United States and Mexico participated in arbitration quite often during this time period, as well. The first of these arose out of the Treaty of Peace of Guadalupe Hidalgo, signed on February 2, 1848, providing for arbitration of future disputes between the two states.

While the most common partners for the United States in arbitration were Great Britain and Mexico, there were many other states with whom the United States agreed to submit disputes to arbitration in the 1800s. And, while the United States was the state that made the most frequent use of arbitration during the 1800s, there were a great many arbitrations between other states, numbering nearly 200 throughout the century.

By 1875, arbitration had become a commonplace enough feature of international relations that the Institute of International Law was moved to recommend regulations for international tribunals. To make clear when recourse to arbitration (then the most advanced form of third-party dispute resolution) was to be had, the Institute, in its report, felt compelled to extend its remarks to the contemporary state of the justiciability question:

> However, it is difficult to imagine that sovereign States, and especially the great Powers, will ever consent, in advance and for all possible cases, to submit to the awards of an arbitral tribunal. Political disputes of a complex nature, in which questions of nationality, of the equality of rights, of supremacy, constitute either the substance or the latent, but real, cause of the difference—such disputes, we say, which by their very nature are not so much questions of law as of power, will always be withheld from such a mode of settlement. Never will

States possessing any power of resistance bow before a judge when
their supreme, or reputed supreme, interests are at stake.[5]

The Institute went on to define legal disputes in the words that were to become
the most often used—that is, legal disputes were disputes that could be decided
by principles of international law.

In 1890, a Conference of American States was held in Washington, with the
express purpose of signing a multilateral arbitration treaty. The treaty was
signed by the representatives of eleven American states, but never entered into
force. While the treaty never became a reality, it is noteworthy in its attempt
to create a list of arbitrable disputes, those being: "all controversies concerning
diplomatic and consular privileges, boundaries, territories indemnities, the right
of navigation, and the validity, construction and enforcement of treaties."[6]

In most of the arbitrations of the nineteenth century, the process by which
arbitration was instigated was the same as the example set by the arbitrations of
the Jay Treaty. In other words, in each instance the parties concluded a special
treaty, or *compromis*, setting up the arbitration and the rules under which it
would operate. Compromissory clauses were also included in certain of the
multilateral treaties of the latter half of the 1800s, including the Universal Postal
Convention of October 9, 1874, the General Act of Brussels of July 2, 1890,
and the Convention on Railway Freight Transportation of October 14, 1890.

General arbitration treaties did not stir much interest in the world's capitals.
The major exceptions to this aversion to general arbitration treaties were the
Latin American states. But even these treaties had so little strength, that "it is
difficult to think of them as compulsory."[7] Indeed, the Latin American states
were so adept at avoiding arbitration obligations that Cory could find very few
actual decisions prior to 1880.

This paucity of general arbitration treaties was to change as a result of the
Hague Peace Conferences of 1899 and 1907. In 1898, moved more by a fear
of the increasing stockpiles of armaments on the European continent and the
attendant cost of staying at parity with other states than by a purely altruistic
concern for world peace, Czar Nicholas II issued a call for a conference to
discuss limits on the arms race and peaceful means of dispute resolution. Even
in its embryonic stage, in the Russian note of December 30 proposing the
conference's program, there is expressed the understanding that political issues
would not be under examination (so as to allay the fears of prospective
participants). The Russian note states:

It is well understood that all questions concerning the political
relations of States, and order of things established by treaties, as in
general all questions which do not directly fall within the programme
adopted by the Cabinets, must be absolutely excluded from the
deliberations of the conference.[8]

In anticipation of the conference, the Russian delegation prepared a draft convention, which drew the distinction between legal and political issues what would hold sway over the conference. In extensive explanatory memorandums on the various proposed articles, the Russians wrote that:

> There is no doubt that arbitration, generally speaking, is a more effective and more radical method than mediation; but arbitration, being of a legal nature, its application is essentially and even exclusively restricted to cases where there is a conflict of international rights, while mediation, although of a political character, is equally applicable to the conflicts of interests which most often threaten peace among nations.[9]

Their memorandum went further, in a very traditional manner, contending that nations could not be expected to submit to compulsory arbitration where interests or national honor were at risk. However, all of this was part of a cautious but purposeful buildup toward suggesting compulsory arbitration for certain categories of disputes including pecuniary damages and the interpretation of treaties related to posts and telegraphs, railroads, certain types of navigation concerns, inheritance, exchange of prisoners, marking boundaries, and artistic property, among other things.

The Russians' plan did not work. There were no disputes the delegates to this conference were willing to agree were appropriate for compulsory arbitration. Certainly, one obstacle was the unanimity rule adopted by the conference, so that even where there was a majority sentiment in favor of submitting certain subjects to compulsory arbitration, nothing could be agreed upon for inclusion in a treaty because at least one state would dissent. For example, the following seven subjects were considered appropriate for arbitration by 31 votes in favor, 8 votes against, and 5 abstentions: reciprocal free aid to the indigent sick, international protection of workmen, means of preventing collisions at sea, weights and measures, measurement of vessels, wages and estates of deceased seamen, and pecuniary claims where the indemnity is recognized by the disputants.[10] But, of course, the main obstacle to agreement on a list was the zealousness of the delegates in protecting their respective states' sovereignty.

All that the delegates to the Hague Conference of 1899 could manage to achieve consensus on was, as Hudson put it, "a codification of the law of pacific settlement up to that time."[11] The result was that Article 16 of the 1899 Convention read:

> In questions of a legal nature, and especially in the interpretation or application of international conventions, arbitration is recognized by the signatory Powers as the most effective, and at the same time the most equitable, means of settling disputes which diplomacy has failed to settle.[12]

This is at once both a weak endorsement of arbitration and a drawing of the line between legal and political disputes. Unfortunately, the Hague Conference of 1907 went no further. In fact, Article 38 of that Convention read exactly the same as the just-quoted Article 16 of the 1899 Convention. The states held rigidly to the status quo, refusing to budge an inch on conceding any sovereignty to third-party dispute resolution. The main results of the 1907 Conference were that some minor revisions were made to the 1899 Convention, and those states invited to the second conference but not the first were allowed to accede to the provisions of the 1899 Convention.[13]

While the results could be looked at in a negative light, that the states could agree on any endorsement of arbitration was a boost to the procedure. The 1899 Convention did achieve some positive results with the creation of the Permanent Court of Arbitration and the agreement on a code of arbitral procedure. Following this modest step, arbitration reached its zenith over the next two decades, measured in both number of treaties and number of disputes referred to a tribunal. This was due in great measure to the stimulation of the Hague Conferences.

In fact, what followed after the Hague Conference of 1899 was a hectic period of arbitration treaty writing, lasting up to World War I, with over a hundred treaties patterned after the legal/political distinction drawn by the Hague Convention. The first of these treaties was that between Great Britain and France of October 14, 1903, providing in Article 1:

> Differences which may arise of a legal nature, or relating to the interpretation of treaties existing between the two contracting parties, and which it may not have been possible to settle by diplomacy, shall be referred to the Permanent Court of Arbitration established at The Hague by the Convention of 29 July 1899, provided, nevertheless, that they do not affect the vital interests, the independence, or the honour of the two contracting States, and do not concern the interests of third Parties.[14]

Between 1903 and World War I, there were over 100 treaties concluded that were modeled after this British-French treaty, including 16 more by Great Britain itself. Also included in this number were 25 treaties concluded by the United States in 1908, referred to as the Root treaties (after Secretary of State Elihu Root).

Under the terms of these treaties, the decision with regard to which issues were legal and which were not lay with the contracting states, leaving room for disagreement that would effectively bar arbitration. This would not have been the case under the terms of two treaties concluded by the United States with

Great Britain and France in 1911. Article 3 of both these treaties provided for a Joint High Commission of Inquiry to settle disagreements over justiciability—this process attempted to maintain objectivity in the decision-making process. The decision whether disputes were legal or non-legal was in the hands of a third party. That Great Britain, France, and the American executive had agreed to this provision was important, and commented upon extensively in the international law literature, bestowing a certain air of authority upon the treaties.[15] In fact, they would serve as the model for treaties concluded by the United States at the end of the 1920s (treated below). These two treaties from 1911, however, never entered into force, because the provision surrendering the justiciability question to a high commission could not pass the advice and consent process of the U.S. Senate.

This period of time, from 1900 until World War I, saw a great deal of tribunal activity, both from the Permanent Court of Arbitration and from special tribunals. But in these cases, there is no evidence of the tribunals themselves speaking to the issue of justiciability. As will be discussed later, the chief reason for this is that in arbitration the disputants have, as a rule, already decided on that issue by the time a case is submitted to a tribunal. Cory found that most of the arbitrations of this time period were *ad hoc*. In only 20 cases was there a compulsory arbitration treaty in existence between the disputants, but these treaties served as the basis for the arbitration in only seven of the 20 cases—and in none of those seven cases did the respondent attempt to refuse arbitration by claiming the dispute was a political question.[16]

After World War I, the number of cases actually submitted to arbitration diminished as a result of the creation of the Permanent Court of International Justice. On the other hand, the number of additional treaties that included arbitration as a suggested tool of dispute resolution increased.

The vast majority of arbitration treaties concluded before World War I almost uniformly drew a line between legal and non-legal issues, and issues that were legal were submitted to arbitration. What was to change after the war was that a number of different formulas appeared concerning the legal/non-legal dichotomy, including formulas which drew no distinction, and arbitration ranged back and forth between assignment to legal or political issues.

One path chosen by states to deal with the matter was the familiar one of the pre-war treaties. In other words, justiciable disputes were defined as differences of a legal nature, exempting vital interests, independence, or honor. A great number of treaties that were concluded before the war were later simply prolonged without changes. In addition to these, there were new treaties concluded after the war that followed the old formula.[17]

Treaties of the above pattern, concluded both before and after the war, were highly subjective in nature. There was a distinction drawn between legal and non-legal issues, but there was never any mention made of how to judge between these categories or who would make the determination. Immediately after the war, such an attempt was made in Article 13 of the Covenant of the League of Nations and subsequently in Article 36 of the Statute of the Permanent Court of International Justice. Even though these will be the subject of Chapter 4, they are raised here because a number of arbitration treaties were later modeled after their provisions. These articles defined justiciable disputes as those falling under one of the four categories said to mark the boundaries of public international law. These categories were:

a. the interpretation of a treaty
b. any question of international law
c. the existence of any fact which, if established, would constitute a breach of an international obligation
d. the nature or extent of the reparation to be made for the breach of an international obligation

Another set of treaties went beyond mimicking the Covenant and Statute's enumeration of justiciable disputes. These treaties would follow a formula established by the arbitration treaties of Locarno, signed on October 16, 1925, between Germany and Belgium, Germany and Czechoslovakia, Germany and France, and Germany and Poland. Utilizing the German-Belgium treaty as an example, Article 1 reads:

> All disputes of every kind between Germany and Belgium with regard to which the Parties are in conflict as to their respective rights, and which it may not be possible to settle amicably by the normal methods of diplomacy, shall be submitted for decision either to an arbitral tribunal or to the Permanent Court of International Justice, as laid down hereafter. It is agreed that the disputes referred to above include in particular those mentioned in Article 13 of the Covenant of the League of Nations.[18]

Reference is made to the list of justiciable disputes contained in the League Covenant, but by that point these treaties have already turned that list into a subset of "all disputes." In other words, Article 36 of the Court's Statute is more circumscribed than the subject matter grant contained here in the Locarno treaties. These treaties do have an expanded view of arbitrable disputes. Having said that, however, "respective rights" should still be read as synonymous with legal disputes, and these treaties do differentiate these from non-legal disputes. For the settlement of these non-legal disputes, these treaties set up an elaborate conciliation process, including creation of a Permanent Conciliation Commission. This raises a further limitation. Drawing the distinction between the two categories appears still to have been left to *ad hoc* decision making.

There were quite a few other treaties of the 1920s that were modeled directly after the Locarno treaties. There were also several modeled on the Locarno treaties which actually substituted the phrase "of a legal nature" for the phrase "as to their respective rights," contained in the original treaty.

There is another set of treaties that Habicht and Lauterpacht both refer to as the American Formula. The first of these was with France, signed on February 6, 1928. Article 2 read:

> All differences relating to international matters in which the High Contracting Parties are concerned by virtue of a claim of right made by one against the other under treaty or otherwise . . . and which are justiciable in their nature by reason of being susceptible of decision by the application of the principles of law or equity, shall be submitted to the Permanent Court of Arbitration . . . or to some other competent tribunal, as shall be decided in each case by special agreement.[19]

This repeats the formula of the unratified treaties of 1911 (United States-Great Britain, United States-France), with regard to justiciability. There is the twofold requirement that 1) a claim of a right be put forward that 2) is consistent with principles of law. Additionally, there is language protecting the advice and consent rights of the U.S. Senate, requiring a two-thirds majority to pass a special *compromis* in every dispute. Further, there are substantial reservations to the basic commitment including matters within the domestic jurisdiction of either of the parties, matters involving third parties, or matters with regard to any subject covered by the Monroe Doctrine. As Oppenheim states, these treaties are "treaties of obligatory obligation in name only."[20] This formula was repeated in a number of treaties concluded by the United States in 1928 and 1929. It is a formula closely repeated in the General Treaty of Inter-American Arbitration, signed by most of the states of North and South America on January 5, 1929.

There were also quite a few dispute settlement treaties concluded under which all disputes were to be considered justiciable. (Immediately, a caveat should be issued that even among these there were certain reservations made, a point to be examined below.) As an example of this set of treaties, the treaty signed by France and Luxemburg on October 27, 1927, read, in Article 2:

> All disputes between the High Contracting Parties, whatever may be their origin, of which it has proved impossible to reach a friendly settlement by the ordinary diplomatic procedure, shall be submitted for judgement either to the arbitral tribunal or to the Permanent Court of International Justice, as hereinafter provided.[21]

Some treaties were concluded under which all disputes were to be considered justiciable and no reservations were allowed for at all. For example, Article 1 of the Treaty of Arbitration between Austria and Hungary of April 10, 1923, read:

> The High Contracting Parties undertake that, in the event of any dispute arising between them in the future, they will first of all endeavour to reach an agreement by means of a friendly understanding.
>
> If, however, it should prove impossible in this way to settle the dispute, no matter what its nature may be, it shall be submitted, after an agreement has been reached by the two Parties, to an arbitrator or arbitrators specially appointed for the purpose.[22]

And, yet, even in treaties that were to be regarded as among the most progressive on subject matter, one can see that a *compromis* was still required between the parties before the dispute could move on to arbitration.

Finally, mention should be made of the last important treaty of this time period, the General Act for the Pacific Settlement of International Disputes, adopted by the Ninth Assembly of the League of Nations on September 26, 1928. The General Act does provide for the pacific settlement of all disputes, either through conciliation, adjudication, or arbitration. However, as sweeping as that sounds, again the distinction between legal and non-legal issues is made. Article 17 submits to the Permanent Court, or to arbitration if the parties so agree, any disputes "with regard to which the parties are in conflict as to their respective rights." One provision of the General Act does have import here, however. The possible reservations allowed for were strictly limited to any falling within the classes of reservations enumerated within the Act itself. Thus, reservations phrased as indeterminately as "vital interests" were not permitted, though comprehensive reservations of the type eventually made by Great Britain and France excluding disputes over any events occurring during any war were not excluded.

A less direct method for identifying the state of the justiciability question during this time period is to note the various systems provided for in the treaties for settling different kinds of disputes. Habicht sorted through the treaties concluded or renewed between the end of World War I and 1931, and arrived at the following eleven systems that were set up:

1. arbitration of legal disputes
2. compulsory adjudication of legal disputes
3. arbitration of all disputes
4. arbitration of legal disputes and investigation of all other disputes
5. arbitration of legal disputes and conciliation of all other disputes
6. compulsory adjudication of claims of right and conciliation in all other disputes

7. compulsory adjudication of legal disputes and conciliation followed by arbitration in all other disputes
8. conciliation followed by arbitration in all disputes
9. conciliation in all disputes followed by compulsory adjudication on legal disputes
10. conciliation in all disputes followed by compulsory adjudication of legal disputes and arbitration of non-legal disputes
11. conciliation followed by compulsory adjudication in all disputes.

Habicht's list is interesting, as it highlights the near anarchy among the treaties in dealing with this issue (setting aside Lauterpacht's insistence that the major treaties can be condensed into a less congested rubric). There is certainly nothing akin to a *universal* state practice. On the other hand, it is the case that those treaties providing for settlement of *all* disputes were very few in number. Most do make the distinction between legal and non-legal disputes.

Most of these treaties, including most of the so-called comprehensive treaties, also contain significant reservations. These reservations undercut the effectiveness of the treaty, and further indicate the unwillingness of states to settle differences before third parties. Most prominent among these reservations were provisions to exclude disputes concerning: vital interests, independence, and honor; the Monroe Doctrine; the Covenant of the League of Nations; territorial integrity; constitutional principles; interests of third parties; matters solely within domestic jurisdiction; procedures before national courts; and disputes belonging to the past. In its treaty survey, the League's Secretariat also noted another reservation that was unique to the time period, regarding disputes arising out of the events of World War I. The Secretariat noted that these were excepted from legal procedure "on account of their general political importance."[23]

One other consideration may be pulled from Habicht's categorization effort, and this is an observation regarding arbitration's changing role vis-á-vis the legal/political dichotomy. Prior to the creation of the Permanent Court of International Justice, arbitration had been the most advanced form of dispute resolution, so naturally it was reserved for "legal" disputes. After the advent of adjudication, there were treaties that submitted legal disputes to adjudication, and placed arbitration into the same hopper with mediation and conciliation, reserved for non-legal disputes. Certainly this was envisioned by the framers of the General Act of 1928, as well as by the states concluding many of the bilateral treaties Habicht studied.

Many of the conclusions drawn about the previously discussed treaties may be applied to the treaties for the pacific settlement of disputes concluded all the way to the present. For instance, regarding the patterns set by treaties, the United Nations 1949 survey of these treaties stated:

The treaties for the pacific settlement of international disputes which were concluded between 1928 and 1948 do not conform to one general pattern, and only in some instances is it possible to find a number of treaties which copy closely a basic model. In most cases, one discovers the influence of several basic types of treaties, which have been combined in a new and different pattern.[24]

What should be highlighted in that statement is the continued absence of a pattern in the treaties. In 1949, the United Nations undertook the same type of categorization of the various systems provided for in the treaties for settling different kinds of disputes that Habicht used. Instead of eleven systems of dispute settlement, the U.N. found sixteen. And again, it may be said that among these treaties, few did not distinguish between legal and non-legal disputes. Among those that did not draw the distinction, most still limited the impact of the "all disputes" language by numerous reservations. Most of the same reservations as Habicht noted for those treaties under his examination remain. As well, the same phrases appear when it comes to including a certain class of disputes, including "legal disputes," "disputes of a legal character," "points of law," or "respective rights." State practice on this issue stood still, as opposed to evolving toward more expansive use of third-party resolution of disputes.

There were general treaties for the pacific resolution of disputes concluded during the period under examination in the United Nations survey, including the Inter-American Treaty of 1929 and the American Treaty of Pacific Settlement (Bogota Pact) of 1948. These treaties obligated the signatories to settle disputes by pacific means, but discriminated among those settlement procedures by the nature of the dispute, legal versus non-legal.

In 1966, the United Nations published another survey of treaties for the pacific resolution of disputes. One thing that is readily apparent to the reader is that it only listed 46 treaties, some of which were simply renewals of previously concluded treaties. For example, on April 28, 1949, the United Nations revised the 1928 General Act for the Pacific Settlement of International Disputes to take into account the change of supranational organizations from the League of Nations and the PCIJ to the United Nations and the ICJ. Most of the other treaties listed were treaties of friendship or amity, with dispute resolution clauses included.

Certainly, the conclusion of treaties specifically dealing with dispute resolution fell off dramatically during the second half of the century. The notable exception was the European Convention for the Peaceful Settlement of Disputes, signed on April 29, 1957. And, in this treaty too, there is a distinction drawn in Article 1 between legal and non-legal disputes, the nature of legal disputes being those four classes enumerated in Article 36(2) of the Statute of the ICJ. Legal disputes shall be submitted to the International Court of Justice. All other disputes (non-legal) shall be submitted to conciliation or arbitration.

On the other hand, in recent years there has been a significant and steady increase in the number of bilateral and multilateral treaties concluded by states. These treaties cover a wide range of topics, but have one thing in common: the inclusion of comprommisory clauses referring disputes to some form of settlement process, very often favoring arbitration over adjudication. Sohn lists several reasons for this, including choice regarding the arbitrators, ability to fit the procedure to the needs of the particular dispute, the danger of exaggerating the importance of a dispute by raising it to the level of the ICJ, and the ability of arbitration to handle state/non-state cases, something the ICJ may not do.[25]

The United Nations made its strongest attempt to coalesce arbitral rules through adoption of the 1958 Report of the International Law Commission (ILC), which had drawn up the Model Rules on Arbitral Procedure.[26] The result of nine years worth of work, the model rules were criticized for supposedly replacing the traditional freedom of movement identified with arbitration with a rigid, quasi-compulsory judicial procedure.[27] The result was that the rules remained only draft guidelines that could be incorporated into bilateral and multilateral treaties by amenable states, as opposed to being elevated to convention status.

One debate regarding arbitration has been alluded to only peripherally in this chapter, that being the relationship of arbitration to adjudication as a method of international dispute resolution. Some additional comments should be made in order to have a complete view of international arbitration.

Right up until the creation of the Permanent Court of International Justice, arbitration was the apex of dispute resolution. Therefore, there was no disagreement but that legal disputes were to be submitted to arbitration. This was to change with the advent of international adjudication. Louis Sohn is particularly strong on tracing this development. He notes that not only was there a drop in the number of arbitrations after the creation of the PCIJ, but there also was a concurrent rise of treaties that assigned legal disputes to adjudication and non-legal disputes to arbitration. He views a French-Swiss treaty from 1925 as trend-setting in this regard. Twenty more treaties modeled on this pattern were concluded by 1928, 47 more between 1928 and 1940.[28] And, as I have already noted, the General Act of 1928 fits this pattern too.

From this evidence, Sohn concludes that arbitration had become a lesser form of dispute resolution as opposed to simply an alternative to adjudication. Sohn's position, however, does not go unchallenged. There are a number of other scholars who see no diminished role for arbitration whatsoever.[29] Firm conclusions are hard to reach on this question. Certainly the scholars appear divided.

Sohn, of course, is right about the wording of the various peaceful dispute-resolution treaties. On the other hand, as we will see below, the *Beagle Channel* case revolves around a boundary dispute, a traditionally legal type of dispute. And, in later chapters, the PCIJ and ICJ will be seen handling highly politicized subject matter. The resulting muddy picture probably indicates that arbitration and adjudication are more coequally than hierarchically related.

The vast majority of what has been examined in this chapter on arbitration has been treaty related. In other words, the reader has been exposed to far more discussion of treaty provisions than to decisions handed down by actual sitting tribunals. This is exactly opposite of what will occur in Chapters 3 and 4, relating to adjudication. The reason for this flows from the process through which arbitral proceedings are instigated.

Arbitration tribunals are, by and large, formed through the explicit agreement and work of two or more states who recognize a dispute and consent to have that dispute arbitrated. Some treaties (including some compulsory arbitration treaties) even require special agreements be concluded between the disputants each and every time a dispute arises, before the dispute can be submitted to arbitration. Certainly, there are any number of treaties with provisions for dealing with instances where states disagree over whether the particular dispute at hand is arbitrable according to the provisions of that treaty. In these cases, the power to make such a decision is granted to a third party. Most arbitrations have taken place after agreement by the parties to submit the dispute to arbitration. Before the tribunal sits, the parties have already formulated the nature of the dispute and the rules to be applied by the tribunal in reaching its decision, and have chosen the arbitrators.

It is, therefore, rare for an arbitral tribunal to have to pass judgment on the justiciability of a particular dispute. One does not look to arbitral decisions for statements on the legal/non-legal dichotomy. That decision has already been made by the disputants. Examining the decisions by states to submit to arbitration does yield some patterns. Some trends have been identified in this chapter. States have been willing to arbitrate a great many boundary disputes, treaty interpretation disputes, and pecuniary claims. But as history has shown, even these three categories have not taken on an air of universality such that states would even now be willing to agree to compulsory arbitration of them. Even as much as disputes in these three categories have been submitted to arbitration, or labeled legal disputes, yet there are times when they are still considered too political. For example, even when one just begins to think of boundary disputes as a given topic for third-party settlement, one only has to raise the specter of Germany's territorial claims prior to the outbreak of World War II, or Iraq's territorial claims on Kuwait prior to its invasion of Kuwait in 1990, to see that even boundary disputes can still be endowed with political baggage too great to allow for arbitration.

One recent case that highlights this problem very well is the *Beagle Channel Case*, in which the arbitral decision itself initiated national security worries and claims of sovereignty infringement. The disputed Beagle Channel, including the small islands within its mouth, lies at the southern tip of South America connecting the Atlantic and Pacific oceans, and was subject to claim by both

Argentina and Chile. Under the terms of a general arbitration treaty between the two states, dated May 28, 1902, and a specific *compromis* regarding this particular dispute, dated July 22, 1971, resolution of the dispute was submitted to an arbitration tribunal created by Queen Elizabeth II.

The decision handed down by the tribunal, dated February 18, 1977, drew a boundary through the disputed region, with the effect of awarding to Chile three of the islands in the mouth of the channel—Picton, Nueva, and Lennox. As these three islands lie east of the traditional boundary between the two countries, drawn through Cape Horn, Argentina became greatly agitated that Chile would now have right to maritime claims in the Atlantic Ocean. Argentina declared the arbitral decision null and void by reason of juridical defects on the part of the tribunal.

After much saber-rattling, including the massing of troops on their respective borders, Chile and Argentina finally agreed to mediation. An emissary of the Pope eventually produced an agreement to set up a demilitarized binational zone governing the disputed region.

This case, while not typical of the result of most arbitrations in the least, probably still does serve as a telling indicator of state opinion with regard to placing important issues before international tribunals. Argentina agreed to entrust the *Beagle Channel Case* to an arbitration panel. Upon initial examination of the case, there would have been every reason to expect that Argentina would have accepted the final decision. The subject matter—territorial boundaries—was of a type traditionally entrusted to the arbitration process. As well, there was a general arbitration treaty in force between the two disputants. And finally, under the terms of the aforementioned treaty, a *compromis* was reached in which Argentina willingly submitted this dispute to arbitration.

Even with all of these factors in place, the dispute could not hold onto the label "legal dispute" it had seemingly been given. It turned out that Argentina was only willing to honor a favorable decision. When an unfavorable decision was handed down, Argentina immediately fell back on the traditional code words and tactics used to define political disputes—especially the claimed encroachment on sovereignty. If even a case as recent as the *Beagle Channel*, with all of its possibilities for success before the international legal system, can falter under the weight of national security interests, then can any conclusion be reached regarding the legal/political dichotomy other than that states do continue to draw the distinction and will be unwilling to arbitrate in certain circumstances?

In fact, in the next two chapters it will be seen that states have at various times, right up to the present time, made the same arguments regarding issues ineligible for adjudication—that the dispute at hand was inappropriate for legal procedure.

The League and the Permanent Court Set a Standard

This chapter is an examination of the differention between legal and political questions as envisioned in the Covenant of the League of Nations, the Statute of the Permanent Court of International Justice, and the judgments and advisory opinions of the Court. The possibility of the PCIJ having spoken to this issue existed to a greater degree than for the arbitral tribunal because of the much greater chance of a case being initiated unilaterally under some form of compulsory jurisdiction. What resulted from the possibility for unilateral application to the Court was a greater likelihood of jurisdictional objections being raised by an unwilling respondent. Certainly, one of the objections to be raised was the suitability of the subject matter for an adjudicatory forum.

Out of the peace treaties of World War I arose the Covenant of the League of Nations, an attempt to provide for peace through internationalorganization. In Article 14, the final text of the Covenant provided for the eventual creation of a court:

> The Council shall formulate and submit to the Members of the League for adoption plans for the establishment of a Permanent Court of International Justice. The Court shall be competent to hear and determine any dispute of an international character which the parties thereto submit to it. The Court may also give an advisory opinion upon any dispute or question referred to it by the Council or by the Assembly.

The Court was not created at the same time as the League because it was considered too large a project to undertake at the same time as concluding peace at the end of the war.

Certainly, Article 14 provides the first insight into the subject matter jurisdiction of the Permanent Court. The use of the word "any" here is instrumental. The only modifier to this is that the matter be of an international character, and that both the parties involved must recognize its jurisdiction or that the matter be referred to it from the political organs of the League. Further definition of these caveats would be left to the Court to speak to later in its decisions.

In February 1920, an Advisory Committee of Jurists was charged with the task of drafting a proposed Statute for the PCIJ. The work of the committee was completed in July of that year, and the Statute of the PCIJ was adopted by the Assembly on December 16. It became binding on individual members after signature and ratification of the Protocol of Signature of the Statute of December 16, 1920.

There were a number of issues that produced much debate among the members of the Advisory Committee. Among these issues were the composition of the court and the election of judges, the competence of the Court (it was decided that only states would have standing), and precisely what law was to be applied by the Court.

There was also great debate over the question of compulsory jurisdiction. It was the decision of the committee that it would propose compulsory adjudication of legal issues. This draft was rejected by the League. When finally adopted by the Assembly, compulsory adjudication had been transformed into an optional clause (Article 36, paragraph 2), which states could accept or reject, independent of accepting the rest of the Statute.

That there was a distinction between legal and political questions in the minds of the framers of the Covenant and the Statute was also clear. This being 1920, there were two influences weighing on the committee members. On the one hand, there was the traditional reluctance to concede certain issues in advance to binding, third-party dispute resolution. On the other hand, if the war had shown the nations of the world anything, it was that reserving certain disputes as capable only of unilateral action because "vital interests" and "national honor" were involved were sure prescriptions for war, as there was too great a risk that settling a dispute without third-party assistance might mean settling a dispute by resort to force. The tension between these two concerns was evident in the speeches of the proponents and opponents of compulsory adjudication.[1]

In the Covenant, the distinction between the two categories of disputes, legal and political, was allowed for. In Article 13(1) of the Covenant, the members of the League agreed to submit to arbitration (later to the Court) any dispute recognized by them "to be suitable for submission to arbitration." In Article 13(2) there was the four-point list that would later appear in Article 36 of the Statute submitted as those issues declared to be "generally suitable for submission to arbitration." The use of "suitable" and "generally suitable" was meant to give states the leeway they had always enjoyed in determining which disputes they would submit to binding dispute resolution. Further, the Council, a political body, was set up in Article 15(1) as an alternative dispute resolution body for those disputes states had decided did not meet the criteria of Article 13.

In the Statute of the Court, in Article 36, jurisdiction was granted to the PCIJ over legal disputes. Again, a legal dispute was defined as:

a. the interpretation of a treaty
b. any question of international law
c. the existence of any fact which, if established, would constitute
    a breach of an international obligation
d. the nature or extent of the reparation to be made for the breach
    of an international obligation

Clearly, in the aforementioned debates, the speeches of those opposed to compulsory adjudication had proven more persuasive during the framing of the Covenant and the Statute. In the final formulation of both the Covenant and the Statute, many subjective words like "legal" and "suitable" were inserted to protect the sovereignty of the individual states.

States' concerns over the scope of subject matter jurisdiction of the Court may be further observed in the acceptances of those states who chose to recognize the optional clause of the Statute. States recognizing the optional clause were allowed to submit their acceptances with reservations. The majority of states included reservations excluding certain types of disputes from the purview of the Court. These exclusions included past disputes, national jurisdiction, territorial questions, disputes arising in time of war, disputes related to particular treaties, and disputes concurrently being considered by the Council of the League. Of course, any such reservation serves to constrict the impact of "compulsory" jurisdiction by cordoning off certain issues, most often due to their political nature.

Article 36 of the Court's Statute also allowed for jurisdiction over "all matters specially provided for in treaties and conventions in force." Therefore, jurisdiction was also conferred on the Court by way of a great many of the bilateral and multilateral treaties concluded in the 1920s and 1930s. Of course, these treaties also allowed for states to register reservations which, in number and content, closely resembled the list of reservations made by those states accepting the optional clause of the Statute.

Another jurisdictional grant given the Court by Article 36 extended the Court's scope to "all cases which the parties refer to it." There are no limitations in that phrase—states may consent to refer disputes of *any* nature to the Court. Of the 38 contentious cases brought to the PCIJ between 1922 and 1940, 11 were by way of a *compromis* (i.e., an agreement whereby *both* parties agreed to submit the question).

Yet another jurisdictional grant comes out of Article 38, that providing for the Court to decide cases *ex aqueo et bono*. Certainly, there is wide room for interpretation in allowing the Court to decide cases *ex aqueo et bono*. The term *ex aqueo et bono* is generally analogous to, but not synonomous with, equity.[2] As Hudson points out, this could include "abstract" questions (*The German Interests in Polish Upper Silesia* case, 1926), which might also be "political" questions.[3] As Hudson and Bledsoe and Boczek point out, *ex aqueo et bono* is a broader term than equity, allowing not only that the outcome of the decision or opinion be based on justice and fairness, but also that the process of reaching the outcome may be based on considerations that are beyond legal norms. The PCIJ was never asked to decide a case according to this standard.

One further grant of jurisdiction was extended to the Court, that of providing advisory opinions. This arises out of Article 14 of the League's Covenant. It allows for advisory opinions requested by the Council or the Assembly of the League.

One concession of power made by the states to the Court was to grant it the jurisdiction to decide its own jurisdiction. Article 36 provides that "In the event of a dispute as to whether the Court has jurisdiction, the matter shall be settled by the decision of the Court." As Hudson notes:

> It would serve little purpose to permit a challenge of jurisdiction to be made before a tribunal unless the tribunal had power to construe the attributions of its competence, and to give decisions with reference to them which would be binding on the parties.[4]

The Court referred to this power in *The Greco-Turkish Agreement* case in 1928 when it declared "the principle that, as a general rule, any body possessing jurisdictional powers has the right in the first place itself to determine the extent of its jurisdiction."[5]

From the outset of the Court's existence, then, there was no clearcut way in which to delineate the issue of legal versus political issues. The Court was empowered to entertain "any" issue, but was constrained by reservations and words like "legal" and "international." It finally fell to the Court to have its input.

Through the period of its existence, the Permanent Court of International Justice would be presented with 65 cases. These may be broken down into 37 contentious cases brought by states and 28 advisory opinions requested by the League Council. However, there were only a few instances in which the Court felt compelled to deal with a jurisdictional matter in a way that is relevant to the present inquiry.

The *Advisory Opinion Relating to the Tunis and Morocco Nationality Decrees* was the first instance before the PCIJ in which there was a real dispute over the legal nature of a dispute. The facts of the case are as follows: On November 8, 1921, decrees were issued by the local sovereigns of Tunis and Morocco, as well as by the president of France, imposing French nationality on all the residents of the two protectorates. This would also serve to impose certain obligations upon those residents, including military service. Included among these residents were quite a few British subjects, on whose behalf the British government lodged a complaint with France.

The British position was that Tunis and Morocco were under French protection, not sovereignty, and so the imposition of nationality in this instance was in contradiction to international law. The French position was that this was a matter entirely within its domestic jurisdiction, and Great Britain had no right to interfere.

The British, still holding to the position that the dispute was of a legal nature, proposed that it be submitted to either the PCIJ or the Permanent Court of Arbitration. The French declined, holding steadfast to the position that "questions of nationality were too intimately connected with the very constitution of the State to make it possible to consider them as questions of an 'exclusively juridical' character."[6]

The British then made use of their right under Article 15 of the League Covenant to submit the dispute to the Council unilaterally. France then took a position relying on section 8 of that article, which read:

> If the dispute between the parties is claimed by one of them, and is found by the Council, to arise out of a matter which by international law is solely within the domestic jurisdiction of that party, the Council shall so report, and shall make no recommendation as to its settlement.[7]

However, after further discussions, the two sides did agree to recommend to the Council that the preliminary question over the applicability of Article 15(8) to this dispute be referred to the PCIJ. The Council so moved on the dispute, and thus it was that the Court took up the issue. The question before the Court was thus stated:

> Whether the dispute between France and Great Britain as to the Nationality Decrees issued in Tunis and Morocco (French zone) on November 8th, 1921, and their application to British subjects, is or is not, by international law, solely a matter of domestic jurisdiction (Article 15, paragraph 8, of the Covenant).[8]

The Court set its task as discovering the meaning of the words "solely within the domestic jurisdiction," and defined it as those matters not regulated by international law. The Court was careful to point out that indeed questions of nationality would fall into just such a category.

On the other hand, the Court stated that even in areas not regulated by international law, like nationality, a state may be "restricted by obligations which it may have undertaken towards other States."[9] And, in this particular dispute, Great Britain was claiming, and France was forced to contest, the applicability of certain agreements involving Great Britain, France, Tunis, and Morocco.   When a matter rose to the level of a dispute over conflicting interpretations of international agreements, then, the Court said, it was no longer solely a matter of domestic jurisdiction. It took on an international character, and ceased to fall within the confines of Article 15(8) of the Statute. The Court decided against France.

It may be suggested that the result of this case was an expansion of international law, or the acceptable realm of juridical review, at the expense of those realms reserved by states from such review. This happened through the Court's reading of Article 15 of the Covenant. As the Court wrote:

> Article ·15, in effect, establishes the fundamental principle that any dispute likely to lead to a rupture which is not submitted to arbitration in accordance with Article 13 shall be laid before the Council. The reservations generally made in arbitration treaties are not to be found in this Article.[10]

This latter sentence was important to the Court. Article 15 did not contain the normal reservations of vital interests. That such language was omitted by the framers and signatories of the Covenant impressed the Court enough for it to refer to Article 15 as "this very wide competence possessed by the League of Nations."[11]   It noted Paragraph 8 of Article 15 as an exception to this competence, meant to safeguard the "independence" of states. But it continued on to emphasize that it was *only* an exception, an "exception to the principles affirmed in the preceding paragraphs and does not therefore lend itself to an extensive interpretation."[12]

Thus, the Court had interpreted Article 15 in favor of the Council at the expense of an individual state. And, in doing so it had increased the possible realm of questions the Council could refer to the PCIJ for advisory opinions. This was a decision favorable to the expansion of the subject matter susceptible to legal review and a limitation on those matters considered to be "political" or non-justiciable.

In the *Eastern Carelia Case*, the claim by the respondent was once again that the issue was an internal political issue, not one for legal review by an outside body.   The results were different from the *Nationality Decrees Case*, as shall be seen.

In this instance, the disputants were Finland and Russia. Eastern Carelia is a territory on the Russian-Finnish border, given over to Russia by the Treaty of Dorpat (signed October 14, 1920, ending the war between the two states). Articles 10 and 11 of that treaty provided for Eastern Carelia to be autonomous, but did not spell out just what was meant by autonomous. For an interpretation of that, the Finnish government relied on a "Declaration of the Russian Delegation with Regard to the Autonomy of Eastern Carelia," dated October 14, 1920, and inserted into the protocol of signature of the treaty. This declaration gave greater meaning to just what kinds of rights the people of Eastern Carelia enjoyed.

Not long after the conclusion of the treaty, disputes arose between Finland and Russia over the alleged failure of Russia to carry out several responsibilities it had undertaken in the treaty, including obligations under Articles 10 and 11 relating to the autonomy of Eastern Carelia. The dispute revolved around the nature of the Russian Declaration. Was it, as Finland declared, part of the the treaty itself and therefore contractual? Or was it, as the Russians declared it to be, merely declaratory of the existing situation, and given only for the sake of providing greater information to the parties involved? The Finnish government presented its complaints to the League Council, and the Council in turn asked the Court for an advisory opinion.

The Russian position in its response to the Court was, in general, twofold. First, it declared the proceedings to be "without legal value either in substance or in form."[13] This flowed from Russia's position that this was an internal affair. And secondly, the Russians noted that they were not members of the League or the Court.

This case is discussed here mainly because it was claimed that the dispute was not legal in its nature. But the Court was never able to reach the question of the dispute's justiciability. It never decided if this was a legal or political question. It was hindered by the fact that Russia had never given previous recognition of the Court's jurisdiction, and it was not now giving it in relation to this particular case. In the famous words of this case, "It is well established in international law that no State can, without its consent, be compelled to submit its disputes with other States whether to mediation or to arbitration, or to any other kind of pacific settlement."[14]

On September 19, 1925, the Council of the League of Nations requested an advisory opinion from the PCIJ on the subject of the border between Turkey and Iraq. The dispute itself was between Turkey and Great Britain (as Iraq was under British mandate at the time). A peace treaty between the Allied Powers and Turkey had been signed at Lausanne on July 24, 1923, which set the new boundaries of Turkey, including the frontier with Iraq. Article 3(2) of the treaty provided as follows:

> The frontier between Turkey and Iraq shall be laid down in friendly arrangement to be concluded between Turkey and Great Britain within nine months.
>
> In the event of no agreement being reached between the two governments within the time mentioned, the dispute shall be referred to the Council of the League of Nations.

> The Turkish and British Governments reciprocally undertake that, pending the decision to be reached on the subject of the frontier, no military or other movement shall take place which might modify in any way the present state of the territories of which the final fate will depend upon that decision.[15]

The border questions were not settled by negotiation, and Great Britain finally submitted the dispute to the Council. The actual role of the Council, it turned out, was also a matter of dispute. Great Britain had made known that it would abide by any decision of the Council. In effect, Great Britain was granting the Council the authority to make a binding decision. Turkey did not recognize the same level of authority. Turkey made known it only recognized the Council's recommendatory powers under Article 15 of the League Covenant. It made clear that it did not see this boundary issue as proper for binding, third-party resolution. As one Turkish representative put it, Turkey "could not allow the fate of a great region like the vilayet of Mosul . . . to be made dependent upon any arbitration."[16] Unable to resolve the dispute over the role of the Council, the Council submitted the following question (there was a second question submitted not relevant to the present discourse) to the Court: "What is the character of the decision to be taken by the Council in virtue of Article 3, paragraph 2 of the Treaty of Lausanne? Is it an arbitral award, a recommendation, or a simple mediation?"[17]

The Court received the request, and made known to Great Britain and Turkey its desire for relevant information. The reply, in a telegram, from the Turkish Minister of Foreign Affairs made very clear the underlying precept of Turkey's position with regard to the case:

> I have the honour to acknowledge receipt of your telegram September 26th stop Turkish Government, whilst having greatest esteem and respect for the International Court of Justice as it has stated on many occasions, is convinced that the questions mentioned in Council of League of Nations' Request dated September 19th and regard to which Court's advisory opinion is asked are of a distinctly political character and, in the Turkish Government's opinion, cannot form the subject of a legal interpretation stop.[18]

The telegram continued on, listing several arguments bolstering Turkey's position, and finished by declining to be represented at the Court's session (although Turkey did consent to supply some requested materials and answers to certain questions).

To answer the question put to it, the Court traced the history of the negotiations that produced the Treaty of Lausanne, the intentions of the signatories, as well as exchanges of notes and statements after the signing of the

Treaty as related to interpretation by the parties. The opinion of the Court was that the wording of Article 3 of the treaty and the intentions of the parties to it clearly led to the "conclusion that that clause is designed to provide for a definitive settlement of the frontier."[19]

Having reached that conclusion, the Court was bound to decide what the role of the Council was in contributing to that "definitive settlement"—could it be compulsory settlement? With this, it was moving on Turkey's contention that, because of the role envisioned for the Council by Article 15 of the Covenant, it could reserve certain issues as not subject to binding resolution. The Court found it to be otherwise. While it was true, the Court noted, that the powers of the Council under Article 15 were only recommendatory, that only defined "the *minimum* obligations which are imposed upon States and the minimum corresponding powers of the Council."[20] Extending this line of argument further, the Court wrote:

> There is nothing to prevent the Parties from accepting obligations and from conferring on the Council powers wider than those resulting from the strict terms of Article 15, and in particular from substituting, by an agreement entered into in advance, for the Council's power to make recommendation, the power to give a decision which, by virtue of their previous consent, compulsorily settles the dispute.[21]

It was the Court's opinion that this had been done through the Treaty of Lausanne. As in the *Nationality Decrees* case, the Court had addressed Article 15 of the Covenant and the powers of League Council. And, again, the Court's opinion favored an expansive interpretation of the Council's powers—what Article 15 defined was the minimum powers of the Council, not the maximum. And, as was indicated by the *Nationality Decrees* case, any expansion of the purview of the Council was necessarily an expansion of the possible number and types of questions that could be brought before the Court, since it was an expansion of the possible questions about which the Council could request advisory opinions.

The Court's opinion in this case was unanimous, and was adopted by the Council. The Council made a decision regarding the border, which was accepted by Great Britain and Turkey.

On July 23, 1926, the Court handed down its thirteenth advisory opinion, concerning the competence of the International Labor Organization (ILO). The case arose out of the work of the sixth session of the ILO, during which the ILO took up the matter of night work in bakeries. The ILO, of course, had been created by the Treaty of Versailles, to improve the working conditions of the working classes, in order to provide for the social justice deemed necessary to prevent the unrest that so often leads to war. Regulating night work in bakeries would have fallen under the ongoing process of regulating working hours.

Article 1 of the draft convention adopted by the ILO read as follows:

> Subject to the exceptions hereinafter provided, the making of bread, pastry or other flour confectionary during the night is forbidden.
>
> This prohibition applies to the work of all persons, including proprietors as well as workers, engaged in the making of such products; but it does not apply to the making of such products by members of the same household for their own consumption.[22]

The employers group of the ILO disputed the competence of the ILO to regulate, even incidentally, the work of employers. After much debate, it was decided to ask the League Council to request an advisory opinion of the Court.

The Court accepted the request, and found that the ILO did hold competence to regulate even the work of employers. But for the present purposes, the more important aspect of the opinion was the Court's discussion of its own role in making such a pronouncement at all. In its opinion, the Court evidenced recognition that, as international agreements arise through very political processes, the interpretation of such documents could possibly set the Court up for charges that it was pronouncing upon political issues, not legal ones. The Court made certain, in this case, to highlight this possible conflict, and declared that "the question put to the Court is manifestly a question of law."[23] Its words on the nature of the case are worth quoting at length. It wrote:

> The question put to the Court has been argued before it both in writing and orally, and the discussions, especially in the written documents, cover a wide range of topics, including national sovereignty, individual liberty, and various controversial theories of society and government. If these topics, which have to some extent a political character, and which are constantly debated in national assemblies when the enactment of labour and other legislation is pending, were considered in the framing and adoption of Part XIII of the Peace Treaty of Versailles, this was natural and unavoidable, as the making of laws, whether national or international, is a political act and as such may involve the application of political principles. That such topics were considered in the framing and adoption of Part XIII may be inferred from the express reservation by the High Contracting Parties, as regards the enactment of international as well as of national measures, of their full, free, individual legislative power, carrying with it the exclusive right to determine, each for itself, what political principles and social theories should be applied within the national jurisdiction. On the other hand, the High Contracting Parties must be assumed to have acted deliberately in providing for the cooperation, strictly limited as it is, of the International Labour Organization in the

exercise of the sovereign powers in respect of labour measures, national and international. . . .

So, in the present instance, without regard to the question whether the functions entrusted to the International Labor Organization are or are not in the nature of delegated powers, the province of the Court is to ascertain what it was the Contracting Powers agreed to. The Court, in interpreting Part XIII, is called upon to perform a judicial function, and, taking the question actually before it in connection with the terms of the Treaty, there appears to be no room for the discussion and application of political principles or social theories, of which, it may be observed, no mention is made in the Treaty.[24]

International agreements are naturally political in their origin, the Court said. They are negotiated and based on conflicting interests and values. However, they must still be interpreted later, and that is a judicial function. Certainly, this must be considered the definitive statement on the juridical nature of treaty interpretation—it is a process of law, not of politics.

In January 1928, the Court was asked by Germany for an interpretation of the German-Polish Convention of May 15, 1922, which related to the governing of Upper Silesia. Specifically, Germany was concerned over Polish law regarding the right of German minorities to attend minority schools. During 1926, the Polish Government had undertaken an inquiry into "the authenticity of applications for admission to the minority schools."[25] The Polish authorities had promulgated certain rules for determining minority status that resulted in 7,114 children being excluded from attendance at the minority schools. Further, the parents of these children who then refused to send their children to the regular school system were fined and/or arrested.

Germany requested the Court's opinion on behalf of the minorities. The government of Poland issued a counter-case, Germany issued its reply, and then Poland issued a rejoinder. It was in the rejoinder that Poland raised the objection to jurisdiction relevant here. It was not, however, an objection that the issue was political and not legal. Instead, it was claimed that the German government had requested judgment with regard to a part of the Convention not listed in the Convention as susceptible of PCIJ review. The Court's reply in this case still has relevance to the present purposes.

Indeed, it turned out that compulsory jurisdiction was only provided for in the Convention for Articles 64 to 71, and the Germans were asking for the Court's opinion on Article 72. For review of that article, both parties would have to consent, and Poland wished to decline. The Court, however, ruled favorably on the German contention that Poland's objection had come too late in the proceedings, that Article 38 of the Rules of the Court required such an objection to be raised in the counter-case. That the Polish government had not raised it then must be "regarded as an unequivocal indication of the desire of a State to obtain a decision on the merits of the suit."[26]

More importantly, by indicating its willingness for a decision on the merits of the suit, Poland had circumvented the need to reference the compulsory jurisdiction clauses of the Convention. And as the Court noted in its most famous words from this case: "The Court's jurisdiction depends on the will of the Parties. The Court is always competent once the latter have accepted its jurisdiction, since there is no dispute which States entitled to appear before the Court cannot refer to it."[27]

This case thus served to highlight just how strongly the Court felt about the subject matter implications of the words "any" and "all" in the phrases "any dispute" from Article 14 of the Covenant, and "all cases" and "all matters" from Article 36 of the Statute. The Court may decline to accept jurisdiction in some circumstances, but consenting states may raise *any* issue whatsoever before the Court. For the present purposes, that should be interpreted as holding for politically charged issues as well as so-called legal ones.

Having said what it did in the *Minorities Upper Silesia* case about the nature of disputes susceptible to the Court's attention, one could suggest that the Court moved in this next case, the *Serbian Loans Case*, to further refine that position. By the terms of a *compromis* dated April 19, 1928, France and the Kingdom of Serbs, Croats, and Slovenes submitted to the Court questions related to the repayment of Serbian loans held by French bondholders.

Even though the case reached the Court by way of a *compromis*, the Court still felt compelled to discuss certain jurisdictional questions. In part, this was the due to the fact that this originally started out as a dispute between private citizens. The Court noted that states may take up the disputes of their nationals. But, in part, the conflict over jurisdiction also reflected the nature of the subject matter of the dispute. As the Court noted, the case revolved around a question of municipal law. To some observers, including Judge Pessoa, this contradicted the Court's "true function" of basing its decisions on international law. In his dissent to the majority's opinion, Justice Pessoa wrote that Article 38 of the Statute must be interpreted strictly, and in his opinion the Court must decline jurisdiction in this case because it more properly fell within the domain of municipal law. The Court's answer to this criticism was the following:

> But it would be scarcely accurate to say that only questions of international law may form the subject of a decision of the Court. It should be recalled in this respect that paragraph 2 of Article 36 of the Statute provides that States may recognize as compulsory the jurisdiction of the Court in legal disputes concerning "the existence of any fact which, if established, would constitute a breach of an international obligation." And Article 13 of the Covenant includes disputes of the sort above mentioned "among those which are generally suitable for submission to arbitration or judicial settlement."

Clearly, amongst others, disputes concerning pure matters of fact are contemplated, for the States concerned may agree that the fact to be established would constitute a breach of an international obligation; it is unnecessary to add that the facts the existence of which the Court has to establish may be of any kind. . . .

Is the case altered if the point at issue between two States is a question which must be decided by application of the municipal law of a particular country? . . . the latter's [the Court's] duty to exercise its jurisdiction cannot be affected, in the absence of a clause in the Statute on the subject. . . . The very wide wording of the first paragraph of Article 36, which refers especially to cases which—like the present proceedings—are brought before the Court by Special Agreement, supports this conclusion.

Article 38 of the Statute cannot be regarded as excluding the possibility of the Court's dealing with disputes which do not require the application of international law, seeing that the Statute itself expressly provides for this possibility.[28]

In the *Minorities Upper Silesia* case, the Court had said a dispute brought to the Court may be of any sort. In this case, the Court said that not only may the dispute be of any sort, but further, so may the facts of the dispute *and* the applicable law. In this sense, the Court felt that the governing words of Article 36 of the Statute were "wide", and thus, presumably open to freer interpretation. Once again, the Court's interpretation of what issues were proper for judicial scrutiny was expansive.

The next case to be considered here is the *Free Zones of Upper Savoy and the District of Gex*. By the terms of treaties concluded in 1815 and 1816 between France and Switzerland, these two areas were to be tariff-free trade zones. France wished to change this status in 1919. The Swiss agreed that certain changes in the regime might be necessary, and the result was a declaration annexed to Article 435 of the Treaty of Versailles, which read, in part:

The High Contracting Parties also agree that the stipulations of the treaties of 1815 and of the other supplementary acts concerning the free zones of Upper Savoy and the Gex District are no longer consistent with present conditions, and that it is for France and Switzerland to come to an agreement together with a view to settling between themselves the status of these territories under such conditions as shall be considered suitable by both countries.[29]

There was significant difference of opinion between the two states over just what changes were necessary. France felt Article 435 abrogated the old treaties; Switzerland felt that the free zones were still intact, but just needed improved administration. By November 1923, the French had apparently tired of the negotiations over the issue, and erected customs lines at the political frontier with Switzerland. In October 1924, the two states signed a *compromis* placing the dispute before the PCIJ. The *compromis* was ratified by 1928, and the Court first took hold of the case in 1929. The case was conducted in three phases, the first two being time extensions granted by the Court for the two sides to negotiate a new regime.

For the present purposes, Article 2, paragraph 1, of the Special Agreement is of special interest. That portion of the Agreement read as follows:

> Failing the conclusion and ratification of a convention between the two Parties within the time specified, the Court shall, by means of a single judgement rendered in accordance with Article 58 of the Court's Statute, pronounce its decision in regard to the question formulated in Article I and settle for a period to be fixed by it and having regard to present conditions, all the questions involved by the execution of paragraph 2 of Article 435 of the Treaty of Versailles.[30]

This provision of the agreement produced great debate over the role of the Court, specifically over the limitations on its power. This debate surfaced significantly in the second phase of the case between the justices of the Court, and by the judgment produced dissents from a minority.

The debate was one over the power of the Court to settle non-legal questions. What was to be decided was economic in scope, the Court being asked to eventually set up a new tariff regime between the two parties. *Minorities Upper Silesia* and *Serbian Loans* had shown that two states could submit any type of question to the Court. This decision would show that such a grant must come in no uncertain terms. In other words, the parties requesting the assistance of the Court must specifically, and unconditionally, request that the Court step into realms not normally considered juridical in nature. Otherwise, the presumption of the Court must be toward a restrictive interpretation of its role. Here, the majority and minority in the Court disagreed here over whether Article 2(1) of the Special Agreement granted such authority unconditionally. The majority wrote that states may be free to settle matters in any way they see fit. But they further noted: "Such freedom, being contrary to the proper function of the Court, could, in any case, only be enjoyed by it if such freedom resulted from a clear and explicit provision which is not to be found in the Special Agreement."[31]

The minority, in its dissent, strongly felt that the Court had been granted wider powers by Article 2(1), of the Special Agreement, and that it could move into non-legal waters. The minority focused on the use of the word "settle" in Article 2, and interpreted that to mean that Switzerland had conceded to the Court the power to set up a new regime in any form it saw fit.

In fact, the narrower interpretation of the Court's role would win out. In the final judgment, handed down in phase three of the case, the Court turned back the minority's reasoning. Further, it said:

> The fact that it was felt to be necessary for the Parties in this case to approve so much of the judgment as might relate to tariff exemptions is because the settlement of such matters is not a question of law, but is a matter depending on the interplay of economic interests on which no Government can afford to be controlled by an outside organ. Such questions are outside the sphere in which a Court of Justice, concerned with the application of rules of law, can help in the solution of disputes between two States.[32]

The decision of the Court was, therefore, that Article 435 of the Versailles Treaty was not to be interpreted as abrogating the treaties of 1815 and 1816, and France would have to withdraw its customs lines to their previous positions. The French complied with the decision, and the zones returned to their *status quo ante*. True to its position on its role as a court of law stated above, the Court did not move on to set up a new regime. (Of course, one could suggest that by not deciding, it had decided. By returning the situation to its original status, the Court did, in effect, say what the regime would be.)

The Court had accepted the case, but had limited its role. True, it was not a decision like some of the others in the sense of being expansive of international law. But that only emphasizes the notion that this Court would only apply a broadening view of international law when it felt it had sound judicial opportunity. Like the other cases that preceded this one, the Court was careful to make certain it had a juridical base from which to work. In this sense, its final decision not to venture into what it considered non-legal territory was not a contradiction of the other cases. The Court would accept any subject matter over which states granted it jurisdiction. This case does not contradict that rule. The majority in this case simply did not feel it had been granted that jurisdiction. So it limited its answer to the legal question it found.

The final case to be considered in this chapter is that of the *Customs Regime Between Austria and Germany*. This case, brought to the League Council on April 10, 1931, by Great Britain, was forwarded to the Court for an advisory opinion. In fact, the opinion was handed down two days after Germany and Austria announced that they did not propose to proceed further with the protocol in question. But the opinion was still given, and it is very interesting for the present purposes because of the great amount of discussion carried on in the opinion (including that of the minority) over the politics of the issue.

At the end of World War I, Austria's independence was of the utmost concern to the Allies, and so it was that in the Treaty of Peace concluded at Saint-Germain on September 10, 1919, Article 88 read as follows:

> The independence of Austria is inalienable otherwise than with the consent of the Council of the League of Nations. Consequently, Austria undertakes in the absence of the consent of the said Council to abstain from any act which might directly or indirectly or by any means whatever compromise her independence, particularly, and until her admission to membership of the League of Nations, by participation in the affairs of another Power.[33]

Austria would need significant financial assistance to assure its independence, and after extending that assistance, Great Britain, France, Italy, and Czechoslovakia signed a set of protocols with Austria on October 4, 1922, which charged Austria again with safeguarding its independence, this time more specifically requiring Austria not to conclude any commercial or financial agreements "calculated to threaten this independence."[34]

On March 19, 1931, Germany and Austria concluded a protocol assimilating their respective tariff and customs policies. The conclusion of this protocol "created a political sensation which threatened to disturb European relations."[35] The League Council requested an advisory opinion on whether this new customs regime violated the Treaty of Saint-Germain and the Protocols of 1922. The Court did hand down an opinion, but it was a badly divided Court. The final vote was 8–7 that the Austro-German customs regime was in violation of the previously concluded accords.

The majority opinion began its analysis by acknowledging that this particular case had significant political ramifications:

> Austria, owing to her geographical position in central Europe and by reason of the profound political changes resulting from the late war, is a sensitive point in the European system. Her existence, as determined by the treaties of peace concluded after the war, is an essential feature of the existing political settlement which has laid down in Europe the consequences of the break-up of the Austro-Hungarian Monarchy.[36]

Judge Anzilotti was much more direct in his concurring opinion in explaining the majority's thinking. First, he noted that there had been for some time a movement underway in the two countries to achieve the political union of the two. This was, as he pointed out, "based upon community of race, language and culture, and thus upon a very strong sentiment of common nationality."[37] He went on to note the "great disproportion in the economic strengths" of the two states, and concluded that sooner or later this union would have the impact of greatly strengthening the movement for political union. The proposed union violated the original intent of the previously concluded pacts in spirit if not in the letter.

The minority charged that the majority was overly affected by these political considerations. What was in the majority opinion was acknowledgement of the politics involved. What was missing was "any explanation as to how and why that regime would threaten or imperil Austria's independence."[38] Indeed, the majority had simply moved from an analysis of the three treaties to a statement that the third violated the first two. The minority continued on, distinguishing between the task given the Court and the treatment given by the majority:

> The undersigned regard it as necessary first of all to indicate what they believe to be the task assigned to the Court in this case. The Court is not concerned with political considerations nor with political consequences. These lie outside its competence.
>
> The Council has asked for the opinion of the Court on a legal question. . . . That question is purely legal in the sense that it is concerned with the interpretation of treaties. . . .
>
> The decision of the Court must necessarily be based upon the material submitted for its consideration. Unless the material submitted to and passed upon by the Court justifies the conclusions reached, these conclusions cannot amount to more than mere speculations.[39]

The minority felt strongly that the majority was engaging in speculation over what would be the result of the customs regime. And that kind of reasoning was inappropriate to a court of law. Adjudication is interpretation of the law—no more. For a court to consider the political ramifications of its decision is to go beyond its mandate. With no proof, *a priori*, that this particular regime was *calculated* to threaten the existence of Austria, the Court had overstepped itself. This narrow interpretation of the Court's role did not prevail. The majority did decide against the union. And as Judge Anzilotti wrote, the answer to the question depended "on considerations which are for the most part, if not entirely, of a political and economic kind."[40] As this statement and the statements of the majority noted above indicate, the Court had taken into account more than just a strict reading of the treaties involved.

Over the course of the cases examined in this chapter there appears to be a pattern of giving international law a wide berth. The Court appears almost activist, ever attempting to increase that which was legal and decrease that which was political. But this impression is chimerical, more illusory than real. The appearance comes mainly as a result of the undefined state of the legal/political dichotomy when the Court was created. Relative to that state of affairs, any defining of those boundaries by the Court would necessarily appear expansive.

Eastern Carelia and *Free Zones* should certainly be seen as examples of the Court recognizing its limits. They proved wrong opponents of the Court who worried over a freewheeling court rampaging over the sovereign rights of states.

They showed that the Court took very seriously jurisdictional questions, and examined its jurisdiction thoroughly in every case. The PCIJ would not go where it felt it could not. Certainly, in *Free Zones*, the Court could have ventured into creating a new economic regime for France and Switzerland. According to the minority, the Court had been granted such a right in the *compromis*. The PCIJ declined. That is what makes the decisions reached in the other cases so much stronger. Those were opinions handed down from a Court that was obviously conscientious if not outright cautious.

A further caution against reading too much activism into the decisions of the Court may be drawn out of examining the rules of interpretation that guided the Court, for as one should note in the above cases, most of the Court's decisions were reached through straight treaty interpretation. As J. P. Fockema Andreae notes, the Court was, above all, guided by the natural meaning of the words of the text. If that did not provide an unambiguous decision, reference was made to the intent of the framers. If the jurisprudence of the Court was expansive of international law, it was through positivist methodology. As Fockema Andreae points out, subsequent history was not seen as an appropriate consideration: "it [the Court] is not led by the fact that the conditions and views have altered since the determination, perhaps long ago, of the article."[41] As he further notes:

> Much of all this is not different from the traditional conceptions in the field of law interpretation; it does not move away from the safe, well-trodden paths which the jurists, theoreticians and practical men have made by the work, often interupted, of more than 20 centuries.[42]

Having said all this, the results of these cases also demonstrate that the Court showed a concern with strengthening international law and international institutions when it was appropriate to do so. These cases showed a Court not deterred by political context. The PCIJ did not turn away any cases out of a concern for stepping into the political realm. Whether one wants to contend that political considerations played into the ultimate decision in the *Customs Regime Between Austria and Germany* case, the fact remains that the Court accepted the case.

Actually, for a new institution like the PCIJ, breaking untested ground, in a period when states were still distinguishing so often between legal and political issues in the treaties they concluded, it is surprising to find so few states claiming issues to be political, not legal, in an attempt to avoid the Court. Are there explanations for this?

One possible answer comes from Richard Falk, when he writes:

> In retrospect, the early Permanent Court years provide an image of a regional institution operating within a global framework. The role of the Permanent Court was facilitated by the character of the Versailles

peace treaties and by its tendency to give rise to disputes, as well as by the homogeneous and moderate character of an international society that continued to be dominated by Europe. When conflicts among European countries emerged in the 1930s, the role of the Permanent Court of International Justice declined rapidly.[43]

In other words, there was bound to be little disagreement among the like-minded. As Falk points out, there was more homogeneity among the client states. There was not the overwhelming division that would later mark the bipolar world that followed World War II.

A very large proportion of the Court's caseload was treaty interpretation, with much of that from the treaties that resulted from the war. Jurisdictional questions in those cases tended more toward whether the Court had jurisdiction over the particular articles being disputed. Most of the disputes the PCIJ settled were not of the sort that states would go to war over, that were perceived to threaten national security. If there had been such disputes, there might have been stronger claims against the jurisdiction of the Court. As Falk notes, when more serious conflicts did emerge toward the onset of World War II, those conflicts were not brought before the Court.

4

The U.N. and the ICJ: Continuity and Change

This chapter moves on to an examination of the differention between legal and political questions as provided for in the Charter of the United Nations (U.N.), the Statute of the International Court of Justice (ICJ), and in the judgments and advisory opinions of the Court. As it was with the PCIJ, the possibility of the Court speaking to this issue exists to a greater degree than for the arbitral tribunal because of the much greater chance of a case being initiated unilaterally under some form of compulsory jurisdiction. What results from the possibility for unilateral application to the Court is a greater likelihood of jurisdictional objections being raised by an unwilling respondent. Certainly, one of those objections may be over the suitability of the subject matter for legal resolution.

The United Nations Charter charges the international community with the duty to resolve its disputes peacefully in Article 2(3), which states, "All Members shall settle their international disputes by peaceful means in such a manner that international peace and security, and justice, are not endangered." The "peaceful means" that the U.N. has in mind are set forth in Chapter 6 of the Charter, that chapter devoted to the Pacific Settlement of Disputes. Article 33(1) reads:

> The parties to any dispute, the continuance of which is likely to endanger the maintenance of international peace and security, shall, first of all, seek a solution by negotiation, enquiry, mediation, concilliation, arbitration, judicial settlement, resort to regional agencies or arrangements, or other peaceful means of their own choice.

One notes the inclusion of judicial settlement in this statement, which like the Covenant of the League raises the specter of an international court. The prevailing view in the mid-1940s of the role, and the limits to that role, that such a court could play also was similar to that prevailing at the time of the League of Nations. As one reads through the U.N. Charter and the Statute of the ICJ, one will find the familiar phrases "legal disputes" in Article 36(3) of the Charter and Article 36(2) of the Statute, and "legal questions" in Article 96(1) of the Statute and Article 65 of the Statute. Those individuals charged with the duty of creating the Charter were very certain that there were justiciable and non-justiciable issues in international relations.

Unlike the League of Nations, the United Nations provided for a Court immediately, integrating it into the U.N. as one of that organization's six principal organs. As the first sentence of Article 92 states, "The International Court of Justice shall be the principal judicial organ of the United Nations." It was the intention of the founders of the United Nations to emphasize to a much greater degree than had been done with the relationship between the League and the PCIJ the extent to which the judicial process should be considered an avenue for peaceful resolution of disputes, the main *raison d'etre* for the organization as a whole. By giving the ICJ principle organ status and making all members of the U.N. *ipso facto* members of the Court, those at the San Francisco Conference wanted to show the Court to be a truly co-equal member of the team, so to speak.

But saying that the ICJ was new, and not just a continuation of the old PCIJ still should be seen as more of a caveat than an introduction to an explanation of a brand new type of judicial body. In other words, its "newness" can be overstated. As Lissitzyn notes:

> the desire to institute a new Court was not based on any dissatisfaction with the work of the old tribunal, but on the desire to make the Court an organ of the United Nations and facilitate the corresponding changes in the Statute, The structure and powers of the Court were but little affected by these changes.[1]

The "different" gap closes somewhat when four additional considerations are noted. First, as Rosenne points out, the notion of a Court as part of the new international system was very much on the minds of the founders of the League, and the idea that the Court could survive on its own without a League is fallacious.[2] In other words, the PCIJ and the League should be considered to have been more interconnected than they are often credited for having been.

Second, as Article 92 states, the ICJ "shall function in accordance with the annexed Statute, which is based upon the Statute of the Permanent Court of International Justice and forms an integral part of the present Charter." As shall be discussed below, there were few substantive changes between the Statutes of the two Courts.

Third, the ICJ has made liberal reference over the years to the judicial precedents of the PCIJ. Of course, the reader is reminded that *stare decisis* does not exist at the international level as a formal doctrine, but the decisions of the ICJ have been informed by the decisions of PCIJ. It really could not be expected to have been any other way—"saying what the law is" did not suddenly in 1946 become a search for new law.

Finally, the grants of compulsory jurisdiction given by states to the PCIJ were transferred to the new Court. As Article 36(5) of the Statute reads,

> Declarations made under Article 36 of the Statute of the Permanent Court of International Justice and which are still in force shall be deemed, as between the parties to the present Statute, to be acceptances of the compulsory jurisdiction of the International Court of Justice for the period which they still have to run and in accordance with their terms.

Article 37 of the Statute of the ICJ is similar in effect, providing that where past treaties referred cases to the PCIJ, those disputes shall now be referred to the ICJ.

There is a reason for pointing out this similarity between the two Courts, which becomes evident as discussion turns to the jurisdiction of the International Court of Justice. Much of what would be a discussion of the ICJ's jurisdiction has already been developed in Chapter 3. Most of the proposed amendments to the Statute raised by the Committee of Jurists in Washington in 1945 were of a technical nature, the change in name and Special Chambers provisions being examples.

This observation holds true for the question of jurisdiction as well. A quick comparison of the two Statutes shows off very few differences. For example, according to Article 34 of both Statutes, only states may be parties in cases before the respective Courts. Article 35 is also the same in both Statutes, opening the respective Courts to the organization's members, providing for equal access for non-members, and assessing costs for non-members.

There are both similarities and differences in Article 36 of each Statute. Paragraphs 2, 3, and 6 of the ICJ's Article 36 are carried over nearly verbatim from the Statute of the PCIJ. There is also mostly repetition in the broad jurisdictional grant of Paragraph 1 of the two Statutes. Jurisdiction is extended in both Statutes to all matters referred by the parties and matters provided for in treaties and conventions. The only difference is the addition to Paragraph 1 of the ICJ's Statute of matters specially provided for "in the Charter of the United Nations."

There are two paragraphs that appear in Article 36 of the ICJ's Statute that did not appear in that of the PCIJ, but they are more technical in nature than substantive. Article 36(4) states that declarations made accepting the compulsory jurisdiction of the Court shall be deposited with the U.N. Secretary-General. Already discussed above, Article 36(5) transfers declarations made by states under Article 36 of the PCIJ's Statute to the ICJ.

Article 37 of the ICJ's Statute is different from Article 37 of the PCIJ's Statute, but this has more to do with the incorporation of the international adjudicative body into the overall organization. Article 37 of the Statute of the PCIJ stated: "When a treaty or convention in force provides for the reference of a matter to a tribunal to be instituted by the League of Nations, the Court will be such tribunal." Such a provision in the Statute of the ICJ would be redundant. As Article 92 of the Charter already provides that the ICJ shall be the principle judicial organ of the U.N., Article 37 of the old Statute became unnecessary. Instead, as noted above, Article 37 of the ICJ's Statute transfers PCIJ jurisdictional grants to the ICJ.

In both Statutes, Article 38 lists the sources of the law to be utilized by the respective Courts. The wording of this article is carried over from Statute to Statute nearly verbatim.

Article 14 of the League Covenant had provided for the advisory opinion of the PCIJ upon request from the League Council or Assembly. This same power was provided for by article Article 96 of the U.N. Charter:

1. The General Assembly or the Security Council may request the International Court of Justice to give an advisory opinion on any legal question.
2. Other organs of the United Nations and specialized agencies, which may at any time be so authorized by the General Assembly, may also request advisory opinions of the Court on legal questions arising within the scope of their activities.

It is the inclusion of Paragraph 2 that makes the difference between the two documents.

What may been seen, therefore, is that few substantive changes were made from Statute to Statute. The general spirit of the document, the limitations on adjudication, and the overall view of adjudication remained the same. Major changes in the international community's supra-national organization were not deemed necessary. The same eurocentrist viewpoint held sway. This observation is especially true for the new International Court of Justice. The framers of the Court's Statute assumed the same character and composition of the Court and its justices, the same client-states, and no real change in the nature of the litigation to be brought before the Court.

More importantly, there also was no change in the "basic philosophy of law and judicial thought-ways and conceptions of the *roles* and missions of the Court."[3] The justices of the Court were either Western or had been trained in the law schools of Western Europe. The result was that the judges were, by and large, products of legal positivism.

This legal philosophy is based on the premise that "the particular issue. . . can be, and should be absolutely divorced from its social context."[4] Strict positivism denied more normative appeals to "oughts" and principles of justice or general principles of law. The source of the law of nations was the will of nations, the law found in the actual words, agreements, and practices of states.[5] Hence, positivism could be referred to as the "black-letter" tradition of the law.[6]

Some form of positivism still permeates the international community. States are still hesitant to give free rein to law based on higher moral principles as opposed to written agreements. However, strict positivism no longer holds sway. States now recognize, as do scholars, that both ethics and a fairer balancing of competing social interests must play some role in the interpretation of international law.

Recognition of this new trend in legal interpretation finally reached the International Court of Justice after the *South West Africa Phase Two* decision of 1966. Just as the founding principles of the U.N. as a whole would face increasing pressure from a rapidly changing context, so too the Court's founding principles were not able to withstand the pressure for change. McWhinney thus notes that, whereas it is more commonplace to divide the jurisprudence of international adjudication into that of the old Permanent Court of International Justice and that of the new International Court of Justice, it would be more appropriate to "classify the Court's *jurisprudence*, temporally, in terms of an earlier "classical", *Eurocentrist* era that lasted up to, and through, the year 1966, and a new, post-1966, "contemporary" Court."[7] The *South West Africa Phase Two* decision, according to McWhinney, marked the last gasp of the old paradigm on the Court. Positivism gave way to a new world-view law.

Though this new legal thought did not gain the upper hand until after 1966, it was probably never explained better than by one of the first judges to sit on the International Court of Justice, Judge Alvarez of Chile. Judge Alvarez sat on the Court from 1946 to 1952. Because of his judicial philosophy, he most often found himself in the minority. In dissent after dissent, he pressed for recognition of a new international law, one brought about as he saw it by the new realities of the post-war era. An explanation of this new international law may be taken from his concurring opinion in the 1948 *Admissions* case (discussed more thoroughly, below):

> This *law of social interdependence* has certain characteristics of which the following are the most essential: (a) it is concerned not only with the delimitation of the rights of States, but also with harmonizing them; (b) in every question it takes into account all its various aspects; (c) it takes the general interest fully into account; (d) it emphasizes the notion of the *duties* of States, not only towards each other but also towards the international society; (e) it condemns the abuse of right; (f) it adjusts itself to the necessities of international life and evolves together with it; accordingly, it is in harmony with policy; (g) to the

rights conferred by strictly juridical law it adds that which States possess to belong to the international organization which is being set up.

Far therefore from being in opposition to each other, law and policy are to-day closely linked together.[8]

This may be an appropriate definition of the *new* "judicial thoughtways" that McWhinney observes taking hold on the post-1966 Court. The relevance of these differences in philosophical underpinnings for the present purposes is best revealed by analogy to the activism/restraint arguments that permeate domestic legal debates. If McWhinney is right, then through the *South West Africa Phase Two* decision what should be observed is judicial "restraint" on the part of the Court. In the present context, that would mean that the adherence to a more positivist philosophy constrained the justices of the ICJ from defining "legal questions" expansively. Conversely, the post-1966 Court could be viewed as more activist. In other words, it would be seen as more willing to use itself not so much as a tribunal for textual interpretation, but rather as a vehicle for *progressive change* through interpretation. As opposed to being a separate entity, aloof, and with objectives different from those of the rest of the international machinery, it should now be considered as just an alternative route for states to use in pursuit of the purposes and principles of the U.N. described in Articles 1 and 2 of the Charter.

The justiciability issue under scrutiny in this book goes straight to the heart of this explanation of the Court's behavior. The cases in which the justices had to grapple with the legal/political dichotomy would be the right cases to support or reject McWhinney's claim. Likewise, if his theory proves to have strong explanatory power, then McWhinney has provided an excellent context for analysis of the cases under examination in this chapter.

The new Court did not have to wait long to get its first case with political overtones significant enough to raise a question over the Court's ability to accept the case. The *Conditions of Admission of a State to Membership in the United Nations* case (hereinafter to be referred to as the *Admissions* case) began on November 17, 1947, as a request by the General Assembly for an advisory opinion. The case arose out of disagreement among the members of the Security Council over the admission of five states to the United Nations, all five having been Axis states during the war. The majority of the Council were in favor of admitting Italy and Finland, but not in favor of admitting Bulgaria, Hungary, and Romania. The USSR held out its vote in favor of admitting all five—conditioning its affirmative vote on the first two on also getting the latter three. It was a very politically charged debate, revolving around the increasing polarization of the post-war period.

The General Assembly requested of the Court an opinion on the following question:

Is a Member of the United Nations which is called upon, in virtue of article 4 of the Charter, to pronounce itself by its vote, either in the Security Council or in the General Assembly, on the admission of a State to membership in the United Nations, juridically entitled to make its consent to the admission dependent on conditions not expressly provided by paragraph I of the said Article? In particular, can such a Member, while it recognizes the conditions set forth in that provision to be fulfilled by the State concerned, subject its affirmative vote to the additional condition that other States be admitted to membership in the United Nations together with that state?[9]

The Court cast its task as a request for an interpretation of Article 4(1) of the Charter, which lays out the conditions for membership in the organization. Cast strictly in these terms, the Court saw the case as treaty interpretation. It was still contended by certain participants that, even whereas it concerned the Charter, the dispute was still a political one falling outside the jurisdiction of the Court. The Court responded:

The Court cannot attribute a political character to a request which, framed in abstract terms, invites it to undertake an essentially judicial task, the interpretation of a treaty provision. It is not concerned with the motives which may have inspired this request, nor with the considerations which, in the concrete cases submitted for examination to the Security Council, formed the subject of the exchange of views which took place in that body.[10]

In his concurring opinion, Judge Azevedo noted the still-prevailing opinion that "the abolition of *non-justiciable* disputes has not yet been obtained."[11] However, he also added the following: "By applying an objective criterion faithfully, any legal question can be examined without considering the political elements which may, in some proportion, be involved."[12]

By a "value-free" or "objective" viewing of the problem, the Court had shorn the request of its situational context, accepted the request, and then moved on to the answer. That is, in fact, exactly how the opinion was literally written. After the above-quoted nod to the objection of non-justiciability, the Court thereafter never dealt with anything but the text of the U.N. Charter.

The Court analyzed Article 4 and found that the requirements for membership were written in such a way so as to preclude any other requirements. States were not permitted to make their consent to membership dependent on any other conditions.

The dissent by Judges Basdevant, Winiarski, McNair, and Read did not challenge the ability of the Court to accept the request, only the final answer given. They, too, stuck to a textual examination, and found that the requirements of Article 4 regarding membership were not maximum, but allowed for other considerations. Only in Judge Zoricic's dissenting opinion was there dissent as to the justiciability of the question. Judge Zoricic could not separate the political debate from the question that eventually emerged. As he noted:

> the request for an opinion had its origin in a divergence of views that arose in the Security Council as to the attitudes adopted by Members of the Council during the discussion on the admission of certain States. These were views expressed in a political body relating essentially to political acts, and based on arguments and appreciations of a political nature. . . .
>
> And although the Court has stated that it only considers the question in the abstract, the reply will, in my view, be interpreted as containing a judgment on the action of members of the Security Council. The Court is thus drawn on to the slippery ground of politics, and its reply may well become an instrument in political disputes between States.[13]

This opinion did not sway the rest of the Court.

The Court had handled its first politically charged case and its first objection as to justiciability by stripping the question down to its textual essentials. The final result, however, had no impact on the position of the Soviet Union. As Lissitzyn notes, it really could not have been expected to have, as states are not actually required to give the reasons for their votes. "Nothing was gained by the submission of the question to the Court. Motives cannot be judicially controlled."[14]

Debate over the admission of new members appeared on the Court's docket again in 1950, and again it was the result of a Soviet veto in the Security Council. However, in the *Competence of the Assembly* case, it was the assertion of several of the states that the General Assembly could effect new membership of its own accord. The question put to the Court was:

> Can the admission of a State to membership in the United Nations, pursuant to Article 4, paragraph 2, of the Charter, be effected by a decision of the General Assembly when the Security Council has made no recommendation for admission by reason of the candidate failing to obtain the requisite majority or of the negative vote of a permanent Member upon a resolution so to recommend?[15]

As had been the case in *Admissions*, objections were raised as to the justiciability of the issue. The Court dismissed the notion that this issue was too "political" by referring back to the words it used in *Admissions*. The Court again saw this as strictly a matter of treaty interpretation. The Court answered that the General Assembly could not vote on admission in the absence of a Security Council recommendation. But more importantly for the present purposes, the Court had once again framed its question as narrowly as it could, resulting in stripping the question of any of its political context. Again, it showed that a dispute could be separated into political and legal components, each to be dealt with separately.

As the the *Asylum* case (1950) and the *Haya de la Torre* case (1951) were to prove, the ICJ would distinguish between legal and political not only in determining its jurisdiction at the beginning of a case, but also in determining to what extent it would become involved in directing the execution of its decisions by the respective parties. Both cases revolved around the same set of circumstances, specifically the grant of diplomatic asylum by Colombia to Victor Raul Haya de la Torre, a citizen of Peru. Haya de la Torre, leader of the American People's Revolutionary Party, had sought asylum in the Colombian Embassy in Lima after a failed military rebellion resulted in an order for his arrest and trial.

Colombia did grant asylum, moved to unilaterally declare Haya de la Torre a political refugee, and requested safe passage out of the country. Peru did not accept the situation, and a series of diplomatic exchanges took place, leading eventually to placing the dispute before the International Court of Justice. In Colombia's submission, it asked the Court to declare proper the qualifying of the offense and that Peru was bound to grant safe passage. In its counterclaim, Peru asked the Court to declare improper the granting of asylum.

The ICJ decided in *Asylum* that Colombia did not have the right "to qualify the nature of the offence by a unilateral and definitive decision, binding on Peru."[16] It also found that Peru was not required to grant safe passage. Additionally, the Court found that Colombia had granted asylum to Haya de la Torre improperly according to the procedure of the Convention on Asylum signed between the two states at Havana in 1928.

It is at this point that this dispute becomes relevant to the present purposes. The dispute did not end with the Court's decision in *Asylum*. This was because the decision did not address the question of actually ending the stand-off between the two disputants. This was partially the result of the two states' submissions in *Asylum*—they had never technically agreed on what the basis of the dispute was. As the Court noted in *Asylum, Interpretation*, "one must bear in mind the principle that it is the duty of the Court not only to reply to the questions as stated in the final submissions of the parties, but also to abstain from deciding points not included in those submissions."[17]

This jursidictional limitation is referred to as the *non ultra petita* rule. In other words, the two states had asked different things of the Court, but neither had asked the Court how to change the existing situation. Specifically, they had asked for a treaty interpretation regarding the granting of asylum, but even Peru did not request the Court to order the surrender of the refugee. Colombia contended that the Court had still not ordered it to surrender Haya de la Torre. This position resulted in the *Haya de la Torre* case. At this point, Haya de la Torre was still in the Colombian Embassy, and through the memorial and counter-memorial, the two states asked the Court to decide whether Haya de la Torre was to be handed over to Peru.

What the Court did was to remain true to the task of treaty interpretation it had set for itself from the beginning. As it noted, the previous decision had indicated that Colombia had irregularly granted asylum, which was therefore invalid. However, Peru had not proved that Haya de la Torre was being charged with crimes that would have required Colombia to surrender him, so the Court could not so order. On the other hand, the treaty in question also did not prescribe a method of resolving a situation whereby asylum had been irregularly granted. Here, the Court noted that there are different ways of terminating asylum. But, as it went on to note:

> these courses are conditioned by facts and by possibilities which, to a very large extent, the Parties are alone in a position to appreciate. A choice amongst them could not be based on legal considerations, but only on considerations of practicability or of political expediency; it is not part of the Court's judicial function to make such a choice.[18]

The Court chose not to settle the dispute, only to define it more clearly for the disputants. Once again, it narrowly construed its task, avoiding any contact with the political context. It would only interpret the treaty, and therefore, its hands were tied in the matter because the treaty did not speak to the dispute. After dealing with all the "legal" issues it could, the Court left to the disputants the resolution of the dispute through "political" processes. The Court had drawn a very distinct line between legal processes and political processes, and would not cross that line, even to see to the carrying out of its decision.

In 1960, the Court again showed itself as able and willing to separate the legal aspects of a case from the more political aspects when it gave an advisory opinion requested by the Assembly of the Intergovernmental Maritime Consultative Organization (IMCO). The Constitution of IMCO had established a Maritime Safety Committee, among which were to be the eight largest ship-owning states. The word "largest" presented a definitional problem. Did this mean actual ownership of the most tonnage or largest amount of registered tonnage? This problem resulted from the practice of registering ships under the flags of other states (called flags of convenience) for various non-nautical reasons such as tax relief. Liberia and Panama qualified under the "registered" definition, but were not elected to the committee. The dispute was highly politicized by nationalistic feelings over which states were sea powers and which were not.

The Court noted the political side of the dispute in its opinion:

> The Statements submitted to the Court have shown that linked with the question put to it are others of a political nature. The Court as a judicial body is however bound, in the exercise of its advisory function, to remain faithful to the requirements of its judicial character.[19]

Remaining faithful to its judicial character meant restricting itself to a textual examination of IMCO's Convention. By doing that, it found that the election of the Safety Committee had been improper, and that Liberia and Panama should have been included on the Committee. As for the political aspects of the case, specifically the issue of registering under flags of convenience, the Court declined comment—that was left to IMCO, a "political" body.

Though there were some early experiments with a nonfighting military presence,[20] the more often recognized beginning of United Nations' peacekeeping operations began in the wake of the Middle East crisis of 1956 with the creation of the United Nations Emergency Force. It followed this with creation of another peacekeeping force in the Congo in 1960. The expenses of the former were dealt with easily enough; the same cannot be said for the latter. The cost of the Congo operation was large, and a great deal of controversy erupted over the financing of that bill, "difficulties... not primarily economic or legal, but political."[21] As Lefever noted:

> As might be expected, there was a high correlation between the material and political support of the UNF. Governments are not in the habit of paying for things they believe are not in their interest. Nor are they inclined to supply manpower or other forms of material assistance to operations they oppose on political grounds.[22]

There were thirty-two states opposed to paying for the cost of the operation based on their feelings regarding the politics of the situation, including the Soviet Bloc, France, Spain, South Africa, and others.

The controversy was political, but it was played out on legal grounds. The dispute was framed in terms of Article 17 of the Charter, and the question of whether peacekeeping operations fell under its terms. Article 17(2) reads: "The expenses of the Organization shall be borne by the Members as apportioned by the General Assembly." The debate was whether peacekeeping operations were normal expenses of the Organization. The General Assembly turned to the ICJ for an answer. Immediately, there were objections to the Court's jurisdiction in the matter from among the opponents of the operation, the objections being that the matter was political not legal. The Court dealt with this objection promptly. It wrote:

It has been argued that the question put to the Court is intertwined with political questions, and that for this reason the Court should refuse to give an opinion. It is true that most interpretations of the Charter of the United Nations will have political significance, great or small. In the nature of things it could not be otherwise. The Court, however, cannot attribute a political character to a reqest which invites it to undertake an essentially judicial task, namely, the interpretation of a treaty provision.[23]

True to past practice, the Court had defined its task as treaty interpretation. This served to divorce it from any political context. At least it served to do so in a technical sense and in the minds of the judges of the Court. It did not fully convince those who were in arrears over the cost of the Congo operation. Even after an affirmative answer from the Court, that in fact peacekeeping costs qualified as expenses as envisioned by Article 17(2), the aforementioned states still refused to pay their apportioned shares.

This case was a reaffirmation of the lessons of the earlier membership cases. The International Court of Justice might have been able to cull legal issues from almost any dispute, but states still saw two types of disputes—and in one of those types, a court had no useful role to play.

I turn now to the series of cases that revolved around South West Africa (Namibia) and the status of the Republic of South Africa's League of Nations' mandate over it. It is placed here because while, technically speaking, this series of cases had their first hearing at the Court in 1950, those phases with the greatest impact were pronounced upon in 1966 and 1971.

South Africa's mandate over South West Africa first reached the Court's docket with a request for an advisory opinion by the General Assembly in 1950. This request was the result of much debate in the United Nations over South Africa's refusal to convert its League Mandate over the territory into a U.N. Trusteeship. At stake was supervision of South Africa's policies in the territory, especially review of its racial policies, which the U.N. wanted and South Africa did not. The General Assembly put a series of questions to the Court regarding the status of the Mandate and South Africa's obligations under it. In response, the Court declared that the League Mandate was still in force, and that South Africa was required to fulfill all of its obligations existent under its terms; that South Africa could not unilaterally modify the international status of the territory; and that modifications of the territory's status could be made only with U. N. consent. On the other hand, the Court declared that South Africa was not required to place the territory under the Trusteeship system. Nevertheless, the impact of this case lay in the fact that the Court had stated that the U.N. did have a supervisory role to play, theoretically limiting South Africa's freedom of movement.

The General Assembly moved to implement the decision by creating the

Committee on South West Africa to carry out its supervisory role. The scope of this committee's powers provided grist for two further advisory opinions from the Court, in 1955 and 1956. These resulted from the Court's cautionary note in 1950 that the degree of U.N. supervision should not exceed what had been that of the League. In 1955, the General Assembly requested an opinion about whether the two-thirds voting rule in the U.N. was "greater supervision" than the unanimous voting rule of the League. The Court answered in the negative.

In 1956, the General Assembly again requested an advisory opinion from the Court, this time regarding petitioners from the territory. The League had only permitted written petitions. The General Assembly wanted to know whether oral petitions would be permitted by the Court's 1950 decision. The Court answered in the affirmative.

These decisions did not have great practical impact, as South Africa did not choose to cooperate with the Committee. As well, they do not have great impact for the current purposes, except as background. The existence of these cases does, however, indicate several important things. First, dealing with South Africa's apartheid policies had been on the U.N.'s political agenda since its very early years. Second, attempting to change the political situation in South West Africa through the legal avenue of the ICJ was viewed as a viable strategy.

As advisory opinions, the abovementioned cases were not binding on South Africa. After much debate in the General Assembly, and at the Second African States Conference held in 1960, a tactical decision was reached to bring a contentious case against South Africa to the Court. Ethiopia and Liberia, as member states of the League of Nations, were chosen as the states to bring the case, and jurisdiction was based on a combination of Article 7 of the Mandate (the compromissory clause granting the PCIJ jurisdiction over disputes regarding the Mandate) and Article 37 of the ICJ Statute (transferring PCIJ jurisdiction to the ICJ).

The submissions of the applicants amounted to a request for the Court to find that South Africa's responsibilities under the League Mandate still held, that apartheid was in violation of those responsibilities (and contrary to international law), and that South Africa must end those policies.

South Africa submitted four objections to the Court's jurisdiction. The first two were easily dealt with by the Court, as they went to the issue of the non-existence of the League of Nations. The Court had already made known in its earlier opinions that the Mandate had survived the demise of the League. The fourth suggested that the issue was a negotiable dispute, and negotiations having not been tried, the dispute was prematurely before the Court. The Court dismissed this objection.

It was the third objection to the Court's jurisdiction that would eventually prove to be the swing issue between the 1962 jurisdiction phase and the 1966 merits phase of the South Africa case. This objection concerned the *locus standi* of the applicants. It was submitted by South Africa that its policies did not touch the material interests of Ethiopia and Liberia, therefore they had no standing to bring the case. It submitted that while member states of the League may have been entitled to participate in the supervision of the Mandate through the offices of the League, individually they had no legal rights of their own in the matter. In 1962, the Court dismissed this objection. The Court had already developed, in answer to the second objection, the line of reasoning that as the League was not able to bring contentious cases, the settling of "any dispute whatever" mentioned in Article 7 would have required the intervention of a member state. As for the subject matter of the dispute, the Court stated: "Protection of the material interests of the Members or their nationals is of course included within its compass, but the well-being and development of the inhabitants of the Mandated Territory are not less important."[24]

Thus, the Court had dismissed all four of South Africa's preliminary objections, and the case could move on to its merits phase. The vote of the Court in 1962 was eight to seven. By 1966, the make-up of the members sitting on this case changed, with one member of the 1962 majority dying, one member of the minority falling too ill to sit through the hearings for the merits phase, and a new judge who would have been expected to vote with the previous majority being convinced to recuse himself. This made for 14 justices hearing arguments, raising the possibility of an equally divided court. Sir Percy Spender, a member of the 1962 minority, was now Court President, thus giving him the tie-breaking second vote. The Court never reach the merits after all. The Court decided that there still existed a question of standing that the applicants had to hurdle that was different from the question of standing settled in the 1962 jurisdiction phase. There, the question had been over Ethiopia and Liberia's right to bring a *case* against South Africa based on Article 7 of the Mandate and Article 37 of the ICJ's Statute. But now, according to the Court, there was still a question of standing to be settled, of "an antecedent character," "as a matter of the merits of the case," over whether the two states had a "legal right or interest regarding the *subject-matter* of their claim" (emphasis added).[25]

The Mandates could be said to have had "conduct of the mandate" provisions.[26] As far as the majority was concerned, an inquiry was required into whether or not

> according to the scheme of the mandates and of the mandates system
> as a whole, any legal right or interest. . . was vested in the members
> of the League of Nations, including the present Applicants,
> individually and each in its own separate right to call for the carrying
> out of the mandates as regards their "conduct" clauses;—or whether
> this function must, rather, be regarded as having appertained
> exclusively to the League itself.[27]

The Court found no such separate right for each individual member of the League. Therefore, Ethiopia and Liberia were adjudged to have no such right, and therefore, no standing. Ethiopia and Liberia's claims were dismissed, on an eight votes to seven majority that included President Spender's tie-breaking second vote.

This fine-line distinction between two different forms of standing Rosenne refers to as sophistry,[28] and was decried in the General Assembly and around the world (especially among the developing states) as having turned on political considerations. In other words, the Court stood accused of using legal reasoning consciously to hold fast the political status quo.

The reaction to the Court's decision made very clear that the debate over this dispute was far from over. For the time being, however, the debate moved back to the political bodies. In Resolution 2145, passed in October 1966, the General Assembly terminated the Mandate under which South Africa governed South West Africa, and transferred control to itself. However, it could not affect a withdrawal by South Africa.

As a result, the question was brought before the Security Council in 1968. A series of resolutions were passed by the Security Council in 1969 and 1970 expressing the will of the Council. In 1969, Resolution 264 called upon South Africa to withdraw its administration of Namibia immediately. Resolution 269 reaffirmed the Security Council's determination on this withdrawal of administration, and set October 4, 1969, as the deadline for such action.

In Resolution 276, the Security Council reaffirmed General Assembly Resolution 2145 and condemned South Africa's non-compliance with the previous U.N. resolutions. In paragraph 2, the Security declared that "the continued presence of the South African authorities in Namibia is illegal," and that any South African acts taken "on behalf of or concerning Namibia after the termination of the Mandate are illegal and invalid." Further, Resolution 276 "Calls upon all States, particularly those which have economic and other interests in Namibia, to refrain from any dealings with the Government of South Africa which are inconsistent with operative paragraph 2 of this resolution."[29]

All these Resolutions by the United Nations were ignored by South Africa. As a result, the Security Council decided to try the ICJ again and request another advisory opinion. The Security Council asked: "What are the legal consequences for States of the continued presence of South Africa in Namibia, notwithstanding Security Council resolution 276 (1970)?"[30]

A very different Court decided that the continued presence of South Africa in Namibia was illegal and that South Africa was under obligation to withdraw its administration immediately. It further declared that member states of the U.N. were under an obligation to recognize that illegality and provide no assistance in the furtherance of that administration, and that non-member states of the U.N. were under an obligation to follow the U.N. lead in dealing with South Africa over this issue.

The decision itself is quite an about-face from the 1966 decision. In no small measure, this was due to a turnover in the membership of the Court (only Judge Fitzmaurice remained from the 1966 majority). It also reflected the serious soul-searching over the Court's role brought by the new members. This change may best be seen through the Court's words regarding the interpretive process it utilized to arrive at this particular decision. If there is anything that can be said about the decision, it is that it was not positivist. This was not strict textual analysis. According to the Court, more important in interpreting the "sacred trust" given to South Africa was "the subsequent development of international law in regard to non-self-governing territories, as enshrined in the Charter of United Nations."[31] The Court further stated:

> Mindful as it is of the primary necessity of interpreting an instrument in accordance with the intentions of the parties at the time of its conclusion, the Court is bound to take into account the fact that the concepts embodied in Article 22 of the Covenant—"the strenuous conditions of the modern world" and "the well-being and development" of the peoples concerned—were not static, but were by definition evolutionary, as also, therefore, was the concept of "sacred trust". . . . and its interpretation cannot remain unaffected by the subsequent development of law, through the Charter of the United Nations and by way of customary law. . . . In this domain, as elsewhere, the *corpus iuris gentium* has been considerably enriched, and this the Court, if it is faithfully to discharge its functions, may not ignore.[32]

Unlike the other cases discussed in this chapter, there was no direct objection made by the Respondent that the dispute was political and not legal. So why has it taken up so much space here? In the first place, there have been few cases on the ICJ's docket that have equaled the South West Africa series in political context. There was, additionally, a strategic decision made by the African states and members of the General Assembly to achieve political goals through a legal venue, chiefly because the political forums had proven unsuccessful.

But the main reason for inclusion is that this series of cases does seem to have indicated a shift in the Court's view of international adjudication. Though the Court's 1962 decision sounds consistent with what is being described here as a new judicial process in 1971, it is only so in function, not form. The 1962 decision allowed Ethiopia and Liberia's case to go forward, but it did so as a result of strict textual analysis of the Mandate. There was no appeal to a higher interest or general principles or a need to fit the Mandate to current needs. That was different in 1971. The cases that follow will be examined in the light of this observation, to see if indeed the Court's new view of itself and its role held.

The *Fisheries Jurisdiction* cases from 1974 were two separate cases, initiated against Iceland by Great Britain and West Germany. (As these cases arose from the same set of circumstances and resulted in the same decision, reference here will be to Great Britain versus Iceland.) The dispute had its genesis in Iceland's decades-old concern with the general health of its coastal fisheries. Dependent as it is on fishing for the livelihood of its people, Iceland viewed with growing concern the improvement of distant-water fishing equipment and techniques. As the government of Iceland declared in 1948, "measures to protect fisheries ought to be extended in proportion to the growing efficiency of fishing equipment."[33]

This reasoning led, in 1958, to Iceland's "Regulations Concerning the Fisheries Limits off Iceland," which extended its exclusive fishery rights to 12 miles. Both Great Britain and West Germany took issue with this new measure, but when the Second Conference on the Law of the Sea failed to produce an answer to the fishing rights question, negotiations ensued between the three states. In 1961, an Exchange of Notes between the three states recognized Iceland's preferential rights in the zone in exchange for fishing rights for Great Britain and West Germany.

In 1971, Iceland unilaterally terminated the agreements, and announced an extension of its exclusive fisheries jurisdiction to 50 miles. Great Britain and West Germany both opened proceedings at the ICJ. The Court was asked to declare that there was no foundation in international law for such an extension of Iceland's jurisdiction. Iceland did not participate in the case at any stage. It did, however, communicate to the Court its reasons for not doing so. Iceland declared that it considered the vital interests of the people of Iceland to be at stake, and therefore it was a non-justiciable issue. The Court took note of Iceland's concern by recognizing "the exceptional dependence of Iceland on its fisheries and the principle of conservation of fish stocks."[34] The Court, however, found that this did not override its jurisdiction, based on the compromissory clause of the 1961 Exchange of Notes, and placed the dispute on its docket for a merits phase.

There would be no chance here for simple textual analysis by the Court, because this dispute revolved around the changing and evolutionary nature of customary law. Great Britain held that the law accepted a fisheries jurisdiction (independent of territorial jurisdiction) of up to 12 miles (Great Britain itself had delimited a 12-mile jurisdiction in its coastal waters in 1964). But Great Britain wanted the Court to find that the then-contemporary state of international law did not provide for a state's jurisdiction beyond the 12-mile limit. Iceland held that while that was a generally accepted norm, there was a superceding norm, specifically that of preferential rights for the coastal state with special dependency on its fisheries.

The Court examined quite a bit of evidence regarding the law of the sea, including the Geneva Convention on the High Seas of 1958, the 1958 Convention on the Territorial Sea and the Contiguous Zone, the work of all three Conferences on the Law of the Sea, and state practice, searching for the state of customary law on the subject as it stood in 1974. The Court focused on the concept of preferential rights for coastal states in all this evidence, and acknowledged Iceland's special dependence on its fisheries. But it also noted that Iceland had exceeded said "preferential" right by declaring for itself an "exclusive" right.

The decision of the Court was that Iceland had preferential but not exclusive rights in the 50-mile zone. This was based on customary law. But it went on further to state that because of the Exchange of Notes of 1961 with Great Britain, Iceland's actions were not opposable to Great Britain. The ICJ directed the two states to undertake negotiations with due regard for each other's interests.

What is key to this decision is that the Court's decision was greatly based on interpretation of customary law and general principles of law as opposed to limiting itself to treaty interpretation. Based as it was as much on principles of equity (the word used by Judge Iganacio-Pinto in his separate declaration) as on the contemporary state of the law, it was cautiously forward looking. Rosenne feels the Court was cautious out of a concern with affecting the Law of the Sea Conference. But that is exactly what Judge Iganacio-Pinto accused the Court of doing. He expressed serious concern that the Court's position had been adopted "with the intention of pointing the way for the participants in the Conference on the Law of the Sea now sitting in Caracas,"[35] the implication being that the Court had overstepped its role as a court of justice into the role of legislator. Certainly, Rosenne feels that the Court's decision did impact on the Conference.[36]

The Court had declined to allow Iceland's claim of "vital interests" to overrule jurisdiction. On the other hand, the decision was not really a *loss* for Iceland either, as the Court positively acknowledged its preferential rights between 12 and 50 miles. With no conventions or texts constricting it, the Court had shown itself capable of finding the law even in ambiguous situations. It had also managed to juggle political concerns to give a judgment based on equity, pointing the disputants towards compromise. As the Court wrote, "the former *laissez-faire* treatment of the living resources of the sea in the high seas has been replaced by a recognition of a duty to have due regard to the rights of other States and the needs of conservation for the benefit of all."[37]

On May 9, 1973, both Australia and New Zealand filed separate applications instituting proceedings against France over the atmospheric testing of its nuclear weapons in the South Pacific. In the *Nuclear Tests* cases, the two states asked the Court to "adjudge and declare that the carrying out of further atmospheric nuclear weapons tests in the South Pacific Ocean is not consistent with applicable rules of international law, and to order that the French Republic shall not carry out any further such tests."[38]

The applications made two claims to the Court's jurisdiction. The first was France's acceptance of the compulsory jurisdiction of the Court Statute, Article

36(2). The second was the compromissory clause of the General Act of 1928 for the Pacific Settlement of International Disputes, directing disputes to the PCIJ (and thus to the ICJ by virtue of its Statute).

The French government notified the Court that it was of the opinion this dispute did not fall within the Court's jurisdiction. This was based on two positions. First, it felt that this issue was inextricably tied to its national defense, and issues related to national defense had been excepted from its declaration accepting the compulsory jurisdiction of the Court. Further, it stated that it did not recognize the 1928 Act as still being in force. As a result of these positions, France declared that it had no intention of participating in the case, and in fact, it did not do so at any point in the proceedings.

The Court decided that as of this particular phase of the case (the request for provisional measures), "the provisions invoked by the Applicant appear, *prima facie*, to afford a basis on which the jurisdiction of the Court might be founded."[39] That provided sufficient basis for the Court to move on to examining the request for interim measures. There it found that it could not rule out that it had subject matter jurisdiction as well. Additionally, based on the small amount of information it had received to that point, it could not rule out the possibility of danger to native populations from radioactive fallout. Therefore, the Court reached the conclusion that interim measures were called for, and as such, directed the following:

> The Governments of Australia and France should each of them ensure that no action of any kind is taken which might aggravate or extend the dispute submitted to the Court or prejudice the rights of the other party in respect of the carrying out of whatever decision the Court may render in the case; and, in particular, the French Government should avoid nuclear tests causing the deposit of radio-active fall-out on Australian Territory.[40]

Events outside the courtroom would intervene in this case's conclusion. Between the provisional measures and jurisdictional phases of the proceedings, France announced it was ending the atmospheric testing of its nuclear weapons. On December 20, 1974, the Court voted 9-6 that as the end goal of Australia and New Zealand's case had been achieved, the claims no longer had any object, and therefore, the case was finished.

The minority vehemently disagreed that there was no object left in the claims, distinguishing between the two different parts of the applicants' submissions. To their minds, the Court had been asked to declare nuclear testing a violation of international law *and* to order France to cease the testing. Only the goal of the second half of this submission had been satisfied. The minority still wanted the Court to examine the larger question of nuclear weapons testing within international law. However, this view did not persuade the majority.

The inclusion of this case in this chapter requires some comment because, as a technical matter, France never objected to the Court's jurisdiction on the grounds that it was a political issue. But such a view was central, albeit implicitly, to France's objections to this case.

It was well known that France had, as a publicly stated policy stance, the goal of military independence. The government of France was too tied to this particular policy politically (both domestically and internationally) to allow for any outside interference or stoppage, and nuclear weapons testing was seen as necessary for such a policy. As for its 1966 declaration under Article 36(2) of the ICJ Statute, it appears, as discussed in Capters 2 and 3, that there are words that should be recognized as code words for "political issue." Such words would include "national honor," "vital interests," or as in this case, "national defense."

Certainly, the judges on the Court recognized this aspect of the case. Judge Ignacio-Pinto referred to the "decidedly political character of the case,"[41] and though Judge Petren worried about the presence of nuclear weapons, he also declared that "to exorcise their spectre is, however, primarily a matter for statesmen."[42]

The result is that the International Court of Justice stepped into what was a very political issue for France at least, and probably also for Australia and New Zealand, given domestic concerns for radioctive fallout. This case carried with it the high politics of both national defense policy and nuclear weapons, and yet the Court was still willing to order interim measures and place the dispute on its docket for a jurisdictional phase. In the end, the Court artfully dodged making a decision in the case. In the second phase of *Nuclear Tests*, the Court failed to take advantage of an opportunity to follow up on *Namibia* with another activist decision. But the interim measures phase still shows the Court willing to accept even the most political of disputes, that is, one involving national defense.

The *Case Concerning United States Diplomatic and Consular Staff in Tehran* arose as a result of the United States' attempt to utilize international adjudication to gain the release of its embassy staff taken hostage in Iran on November 4, 1979. The embassy compound had been overrun during a demonstration against the United States days after the United States accepted the former Shah of Iran for medical attention. The U.S. response included quite a few measures including boycotting the importation of Iranian oil and freezing Iranian assets in the United States. It moved on the international diplomatic front by raising the issue at the U.N. Security Council. It also attempted to obtain a juridical order for the release of the detainees by making a unilateral application to the ICJ.

The U.S. complaint rested entirely on treaty law. Specifically, it charged that Iran, "in tolerating, encouraging, and failing to prevent and punish the conduct described. . . violated its international legal obligations" under various articles of the Vienna Convention on Diplomatic Relations; the Vienna Convention on

Consular Relations; the Convention on the Prevention and Punishment of Crimes against Internationally Protected Persons, including Diplomatic Agents; the Treaty of Amity, Economic Relations, and Consular Rights between the United States and Iran; and the U.N. Charter.

The government of Iran refused to participate in the proceedings. It did communicate to the Court the reasons for its refusal in a letter dated December 9, 1979. As the only communication from Iran regarding the case, it deserves extensive quotation here. In part, it read:

> [Iran] respectfully draws the attention of the Court to the deep-rootedness and the essential character of the Islamic Revolution of Iran, a revolution of a whole oppressed nation against its oppressors and their masters, the examination of whose numerous repercussions is essentially and directly a matter within the national sovereignty of Iran. . . .
>
> The Court cannot and should not take cognizance of the case. . . .
>
> For this question only represents a marginal and secondary aspect of an overall problem, one such that it cannot be studied separately, and which involves, *inter alia*, more than 25 years of continual interference by the United States in the internal affairs of Iran, the shameless exploitation of our country, and numerous crimes perpetrated against the Iranian people, contrary to and in conflict with all international and humanitarian norms.
>
> The problem involved in the conflict between Iran and the United States is thus not one of the interpretation and the application of the treaties upon which the American Application is based, but results from an overall situation containing much more fundamental and more complex elements. Consequently, the Court cannot examine the American Application divorced from its proper context, namely the whole political dossier of the relations between Iran and the United States over the last 25 years.[43]

Phase One of the case was a request by the United States for the Court to exercise its power of provisional measures under Article 41 of its Statute to order the release of the detained individuals. The Court unanimously ordered that release (as well as several other actions by the disputants). The interim order was handed down on December 15, 1979, but had no practical effect; Iran did not release the detainees.

The Court handed down its judgment in the case on May 24, 1980. The main thrust of its decision was that Iran had violated its responsibilities to the United States under international law, as expressed both in conventions and under general principles of international law. It then reiterated its position taken during the interim measures phase that redress of the situation must be centered on release of the diplomatic personnel and return of embassy property.

As for Iran's objection to the Court's jurisdiction of the dispute, the Court was swift in its dismissal, emphasizing that the taking of hostages could not be considered marginal to any larger dispute. But, for the present purposes, its answer to Iran's concern about the political nature of the dispute is of particular interest. The Court wrote:

> Nor has it [Iran] made any attempt to explain, still less define, what connection, legal or factual, there may be between the "overall problem" of its general grievances against the United States and the particular events that gave rise to the United States' claims in the present case which, in its view, precludes the separate examination of those claims by the Court. This was the more necessary because legal disputes between sovereign States by their very nature are likely to occur in political contexts, and often form only one element in a wider and longstanding political dispute between the States concerned. Yet never has the view been put forward before that, because a legal dispute submitted to the Court is only one aspect of a political dispute, the Court should decline to resolve for the parties the legal questions at issue between them. Nor can any basis for such a view of the Court's functions or jurisdiction be found in the Charter or the Statute of the Court; if the Court were, contrary to its settled jurisprudence, to adopt such a view, it would impose a far-reaching and unwarranted restriction upon the role of the Court in the peaceful solution of international disputes.[44]

This answer fits the Court's previous pronouncements in this area very closely. Even where there is a significant political context to a dispute, the Court will deal with those legal aspects presented to it. It is willing to separate the two spheres.

At first glance, this response by the Court sounds very much like a pre-1966 decision of the Court. Like those decisions, the Court has separated out the legal from the political. Also, similar to those earlier disputes, the main thrust of the Court's decision hinges on textual analysis of conventions in force. But there are some differences, as well, which appear to make this case fit the post-1966 casting of cases proposed by McWhinney.

In the first place, this decision does not shy away from acknowledgement of the surrounding context. In fact, there is significant discussion of it, and what part it played or did not play in the decision.

But what seems most consistent between this decision and the other post-1966 decisions is the willingness to stray from textual analysis. Diplomatic law is not a branch of international law that is strictly text driven. As the Court pointed out, diplomatic law has a very ancient history. As a result, it has a firm place in customary law. The protection of diplomats is a general principle of law. The Court referred to this aspect of the problem liberally. The Court also mentioned that holding people against their will flies in the face of the meaning and provisions of the Universal Declaration of Human Rights. The Universal Declaration is a document about which there is no real consensus regarding its legal standing. It was not intended to have binding status. Yet many have been willing to suggest over the years that it has finally joined the corpus of customary law. For the Court to have referred to it, especially when it did not have to, spoke to the Court's more expansive view of the law.

This latter point is the important one. The Court did not have to discuss general principles of law. It did not have to mention the Universal Declaration. The decision would have been the same had the Court only interpreted the relevant conventions. The Court's old interpretive rules would have had the Court content to stop there. In this case, the Court clearly felt something was gained by expanding beyond the texts into more general law. What was to be gained could have been as simple as added strength for this particular decision. But as noted, the decision would have been the same just on the basis of the texts.   More likely, this is part and parcel of the trend we have discussed through McWhinney's framework. It is the Court showing just how broadly based is its province.

The *Case Concerning Military and Paramilitary Activities In and Against Nicaragua* had its beginnings in 1979, when the Somoza regime formally relinquished power to the Sandinista National Liberation Front. Though the Sandinistas had originally enjoyed the support of the United States, that was to change quickly due to U.S. perceptions of unwelcome policies followed by the new Nicaraguan goverment.

This U.S. opposition grew to the point where the United States was actively supporting the Sandinista's opposition. This support ranged from simple monetary financing to military weapons and training. By 1983, this assistance had reached the level of direct action by the U.S. Central Intelligence Agency. Operatives in the employment of, and under the direct supervision of, the CIA were responsible for the laying of mines in a number of Nicaragua's harbors and armed raids on Nicaragua's ports and oil facilities.

On April 4, 1984, Nicaragua placed a resolution before the U.N. Security Council, seeking an order enjoining the United States from continuing its activities against Nicaragua. The United States cast a veto of the measure. The Nicaraguans responded with an application to the ICJ. It was a move that was anticipated by the United States. On April 6, it attempted to modify its 1946 declaration of acceptance of the Court's compulsory jurisdiction. This modification stated:

the aforesaid declaration shall not apply to disputes with any Central American State or arising out of or related to events in Central

America. . . .

Notwithstanding the terms of the aforesaid declaration, this proviso shall take effect immediately and shall remain in force for two years, so as to foster the continuing regional dispute settlement process which seeks a negotiated solution to the interrelated political, economic and security problems of Central America.[45]

The Nicaragua case was built around showing U.S. actions as armed aggression in violation of the U.N. Charter; the Charter of the Organization of American States; the Convention on Rights and Duties of States; the Convention concerning the Duties and Rights of States in the Event of Civil Strife; and the general rules regarding sovereignty of states as found in customary international law. Nicaragua requested the Court to declare that the United States was guilty of said violations and liable for compensation to Nicaragua.

The first phase of the case took place as a request by Nicaragua for provisional measures. The United States took part in this phase, requesting that the Court declare it had no jurisdiction in the case. The Court decided that it would address the jurisdictional questions in the case in a separate, but later, stage of the proceedings. Its decision of May 10, 1984, was to order the requested provisional measures, directing the United States to cease its mine-laying operations, and directing that neither state should take any further actions that might aggravate the dispute.

Thus, the case moved to a jurisdictional phase, argued during hearings before the Court in October 1984. Nicaragua based the Court's jurisdiction on the compulsory jurisdiction of the Court's Statute, arguing that by virtue of the U.S. Declaration of 1946, and Nicaragua's Declaration of 1929 accepting the jurisdiction of the PCIJ (and the transfer of that to the ICJ through Article 36(5) of the ICJ Statute), both parties in the dispute had accepted the compulsory jurisdiction of the Court. Further, it noted the compromissory clause of the Treaty of Friendship, Commerce, and Navigation between the United States and Nicaragua of May 24, 1958, also covered the claims presented in the Application.

As to these jurisdictional claims, the United States argued that Nicaragua's 1929 Declaration had never been ratified. It further argued that even if the Court should find that it had been ratified in a way that met the Court's rules, the 1984 modification of the U.S. acceptance of the optional clause barred the Court's jurisdiction. It further argued that the 1958 treaty between the two states did not apply to the claims put forward by Nicaragua.

The Court eventually accepted jurisdiction under both the compulsory jurisdiction of the ICJ Statute and the 1958 treaty. Nevertheless, it still had to deal with several contentions of the United States as to admissibility of the claims. There were five of these claims, but not all are relevant to the purposes of the present effort. Those that are relevant suggested that the Nicaraguan claims were of a nature (ongoing conflict) better suited to political processes than to legal ones. Specifically, the United States contended that the Security Council of the U.N. and the Contadora Process among the Central American states were both apprised of the situation, and were more appropriate venues. This is because such conflict

> lacks the attributes necessary for the application of the judicial process, namely a pattern of legally relevant facts discernible by the means available to the adjudicating tribunal, establishable in conformity with applicable norms of evidence and proof, and not subject to further material evolution during the course of, or subsequent to, the judicial proceedings. It is for reasons of this nature that ongoing armed conflict must be entrusted to resolution by political processes.[46]

The United States referred to this elsewhere as "the integrity of the judicial function."[47]

The Court brushed aside these warnings of the U.S., writing:

> It is clear that the complaint of Nicaragua is not about an ongoing armed conflict between it and the United States, but one requiring, and indeed demanding, the peaceful settlement of disputes between the two States. Hence, it is properly brought before the principal judicial organ of the Organization for peaceful settlement.[48]

The Court decided by a vote of fifteen votes to one that it had jurisdiction to entertain the submission of Nicaragua.

The Court's formulation of the U.S. position, quoted above, attempted to distinguish between the United States calling the dispute a political one (which it thought the United States was not doing) and calling the dispute inappropriate for judicial processes. But if the Court had any doubt about that point, the United States cleared it up on January 18, 1985, when it delivered a letter to the Court declaring that "the United States is constrained to conclude that the judgment of the Court was clearly and manifestly erroneous as to both fact and law."[49] In a statement released concurrently, the United States declared:

> The conflict in Central America. . . is not a narrow legal dispute; it is an inherently political problem that is not appropriate for judicial resolution. The conflict will be solved only by political and diplomatic means—not through a judicial tribunal. The International Court of Justice was never intended to resolve issues of collective security and self-defense and is patently unsuited for such a role. . . .

> [This case is a] blatant misuse of the Court for political
> purposes. . . the Court does not have jurisdiction and competence in
> this case. . . .
>
> The decision of November 26 represents an over-reaching of the
> Court's limits, a departure from its tradition of judicial restraint, and
> a risky venture into treacherous political waters.[50]

In fact, the United States did not participate thereafter. Nicaragua filed its memorial on the merits, and hearings were held in September 1985. The United States gave notice in October, 1985, that it was terminating its acceptance of the compulsory jurisdiction of the Court. In June, 1986, the ICJ handed down its judgment. In its 16 operative paragraphs, the Court decided that the United States' activities violated its obligations under customary law not to intervene in the affairs of another State, use force against another State, violate the sovereignty of another State, or interrupt peaceful maritime commerce. It also found the United States' activities violated the 1956 Friendship Treaty and that all these violations incurred upon the United States an obligation to make reparations.

This case was as politicized as any the Court has ever been seised of, and yet it accepted the case. It took great care to note that significant questions of both customary law and treaty law were involved in the questions submitted to it. The Court also repeated it words from the *Diplomatic and Consular Staff* case to the effect that simply because a case has political aspects does not make it less liable to the Court for its legal aspects.

It is also worth noting that the ICJ accepted this case in the face of serious charges by one of the parties that it was overstepping the bounds of judicial propriety. The United States questioned the Court's view of its role. That role, as the United States saw it, was narrow—an interpreter of the law. The Court's response to that charge, given in its decision as to jurisdiction, formulated its role as an organ for the "peaceful settlement of disputes."[51] It further likened that role to the Security Council's "responsibility for the maintenance of international peace and security."[52] Judge Alvarez would have approved of such language.

As a subsequent offshoot of this case, Nicaragua felt emboldened enough by the Court's validation of the facts of the dispute to institute proceedings against Honduras for its support of the contras. In this case, the *Case Concerning Border and Transborder Armed Actions*, Honduras entered the following objection to admissibility: "It is a politically-inspired, artificial request which the Court should not entertain consistently with its judicial character."[53]

The Court gave its standard response that it was "aware that political aspects may be present in any legal dispute brought before it."[54] But of itself, that could not bar the Court if the Court found that the dispute before it is a legal dispute, in the sense of a dispute capable of being settled by the application of priciples and rules of international law, and secondly, that the Court has jurisdiction to deal with it, and that that jurisdiction is not fettered by any circumstance rendering the application inadmissible.[55]

The Court denied this objection. In fact, the Court found that it did have jurisdiction over the dispute and it advanced to the merits phase. However, the case was later dropped by the new Chamorro government in Nicaragua.

Two different lines of thought were pursued in this chapter. There was an examination of which cases the Court would accept or decline to accept when objections were expressed due to the politics inherent in the particular dispute. There was also an application of this particular subset of the ICJ's caseload to a theory put forward by Edward McWhinney to explain the underlying stimulus for a hypothesized new era on the Court. McWhinney suggests that the Court has moved beyond positivism, with its greater reliance on textual interpretation, and more into the direction of Naturalism, with its greater reliance on general principles of law and the higher good of more equitable outcomes.

As has been seen, in no instance where the Court was faced with an objection over the propriety of its accepting a case due to its political overtones did the Court ever let the political context deter it from accepting the dispute. This held across both contentious cases and advisory opinions. As has also been seen, there is a nice reciprocal relationship between this subset of cases and McWhinney's theory. These cases have, for the most part, supported his theory, and his theory has served well to delineate two very different motivational eras in the Court's jurisprudence. How these two conclusions fit into the larger point of this book will be seen in the final chapter.

Where Angels Fear to Tread

The present chapter has a threefold purpose. The first task is to draw together the four previous chapters. While each chapter dealt with the difference between legal and political questions in international law, each dealt with the decisions of a separate entity, with little carry-over between the chapters. The result is that some degree of synthesis is necessary. The second task is to determine if the evidence uncovered leads to any worthwhile conclusions about the difference between legal and political questions in international law. The chapter's final task is to discuss any implications that might arise from those conclusions.

Discussion of this subject began, in Chapter 1, with an examination of the scholarship that has surrounded the topic. The first opinion on the matter was traced back to Vattel in the mid-1700s. There, in its earliest formulations, the differentiation between legal and political questions was seen to be self-explanatory. International tribunals had useful roles to play in the resolution of inter-state disputes, but only in a certain subset of such disputes. International arbitration, it was stated, was relevant only to disputes where no vital interests of the state were involved.

That opinion was Vattel's in 1758. But this position remained as the reigning paradigm for a long time, holding unchallenged primacy through the conclusion of World War I. If there were voices of opposition during the pre-war period, they were fairly quiet ones. In the aftermath of war, with the benefit of hindsight, the horror of the war made viable the position that unilateral decisions about security may have brought on the war and perhaps international arbitration and adjudication could have settled the disputes before war broke out.

Adherents of this new position suggested that there was no objective standard for distinguishing between legal and political questions. The greatest voice in this school, that of Hersch Lauterpacht, suggested this was so, not simply because it was too hard to find the division, but more because international law was such that it did not admit of any division. International law should be viewed as a complete body of law, one with no gaps (as has been argued by so many others). The result is that there are no disputes to which international law cannot be applied. This position would be echoed forcefully later by Rosalyn Higgins.

With only a few exceptions, however, this "idealistic" position was the minority one. By far, the more widely held position was the "realist" one—some dispute subject matter was justiciable and some was non-justiciable. Certain disputes fell into this latter category by virtue of their political overtones. This position remained the dominant one even under the pressure of the idealists.

This realist position coincided strongly with state practice. Right through to the present time, with only a few exceptions, states have proven themselves unwilling to completely and unwaiveringly entrust all disputes to international third-party dispute resolution.

Evidence that state practice has been to distinguish between the legal and the political also arises from examination of international arbitration. Of course, as was indicated in Chapter 2, arbitration tribunals are formed most often through explicit agreement by both parties. The actual arbitrations that have been conducted only indicate which disputes certain states have been willing to settle through binding, third-party decisions in certain periods. No unalterable and generalizable patterns arose from the evidence provided by arbitration case history.

The compromissory treaties proved to be a different story. Throughout the last two centuries, the vast majority of arbitration treaties that obliged states in advance to submit certain future disputes to arbitration have made explicit the "vital interest" type of exceptions. With few exceptions, treaty after treaty was concluded which reserved certain issues as non-arbitrable. States showed themselves by their actions to be constantly vigilant of their sovereignty rights.

In the separate examinations of Chapters 1 and 2, one should see the genesis of the legal question/political question dichotomy in international law. Of course, which came first is hard to determine. But whether state practice precipitated scholarly comment or whether scholars pointed the way and provided justification for later state practice makes little difference. Rather, what should be noted is that there has been little deviation from the standard. State practice, as evidenced in the arbitration treaties that differentiate between types of disputes, and most international law specialists were apt to agree that that differentiation was either necessary or unavoidable.

The impact of all this agreement in this context may be seen in the transfer of this distinction to the creation of international adjudication and the two major adjudicative bodies of the twentieth century. The opinions of those who set up the Permanent Court of International Justice and the International Court of

Justice remained supportive of the legal/political dichotomy already discussed.

The domain of the Courts' powers was delineated in their respective Statutes (as well as references made to them in the League of Nations Covenant and the United Nations Charter). Words were carefully chosen so as to indicate that the subject matter jurisdiction of the Courts was limited to "legal" matters as defined by Article 38 of each Statute. Further, the Statutes of the two Courts limited the competence of these new international bodies. State consent would still drive dispute resolution, consent granted through a *compromis*, through a compromissory clause, or through prior acceptance of the optional clause providing for compulsory jurisdiction.

Even in this last category of jurisdictional grant, acceptance of the optional clause, "compulsory" has proven to be an illusory term. States have been able to provide themselves loopholes in the form of reservations. The states that accepted the compulsory jurisdiction of the PCIJ or the ICJ did so making liberal use of the possibility for appending reservations to exclude certain types of future disputes.

In fact, few declarations of acceptance of the compulsory jurisdiction provisions of the PCIJ and no declarations under the ICJ Statute have been made without reservations. In the case of the current set of declarations of acceptance, these reservations range in limitation capacity from the simple condition of reciprocity ("in relation to any other State accepting the same obligation") to the more far-reaching, self-judging nature of the so-called Connally Amendment introduced by the United States (the United States was not the only state with a self-judging reservation among those in its declaration).

What was required for courts of law so circumscribed in their powers was a thorough examination of the jurisdictional basis for action by each of the Courts in each dispute before them. Each judgment or opinion given by the PCIJ or the ICJ begins with discussion of the jurisdictional question. What tends to happen in the opinions is that the judges first address the respondent's question of the "legality" of the issue. Then, having satisfied themselves that the objection over the political nature of the dispute is without merit, they move on to examine the grant of jurisdiction upon which the applicant state has based its claim. Some cases began with a separate jurisdictional phase, with submissions and arguments made on the Court's jurisdiction. Once a Court decision was made on jurisdiction, *then* the dispute was moved on to the merits phase. As regards the cases selected for examination in this book, the two Courts have been remarkably consistent with respect to jurisdiction.

Of the 65 cases that represent the jurisprudence of the Permanent Court of International Justice, eight cases were identified here as marking those instances in which the political context of the dispute was raised as a possible barrier to the Court's competence or the Court felt it necessary to define the dispute as susceptible to legal review. Only in the instance of *Eastern Carelia* did the Court decline jurisdiction over the dispute, and that was not due to the Soviet

Union's objection over the political nature of the subject matter. Rather, it declined due to the larger issue of the Soviet Union's lack of recognition of the League and the PCIJ, and its sovereign right of denial of consent to those bodies' jurisdiction over it.

Therefore, if *Eastern Carelia* is discarded, and the sample set drops to seven cases, the fact is that there is a 100 percent acceptance rate. The Court took all seven cases regardless of the political context (even where it purported to be squeamish about the issue, in the *Free Zones* case, it gave a judgment). Or, put another way, it would appear the Court was *never* convinced that political context was a true barrier to jurisdiction. It was obviously of secondary importance where the Court otherwise found specific jurisdictional grants by the disputants.

Depending on how one views the decision in the first phase of the *Nuclear Tests* case, the same acceptance rate either does hold for the International Court of Justice or nearly does. If one believes that the Court was assuming jurisdiction by its grant of provisional measures, then the Court accepted all the cases herein under examination. If one assumes that the Court meant for its grant of provisional measures to serve merely as a step on the way to considering the jurisdictional questions, then the Court's record is not necessarily without exception. The problem in deciphering this case is that the thoughts of the judges of the majority are not stated. The Court bowed out of the case on a more technical front, claiming that the dispute no longer existed. Therefore, the Court did not have to reach the question of jurisdiction.

John Dugard seems to feel that the Court was very conscious of the political nature of the dispute and very concerned about non-compliance and "committing itself on such highly debatable and controversial rules of customary law."[1] Dugard notes that the four concurring opinions from the majority discussed the political nature of the dispute and the inappropriateness of the Court pronouncing in such an area. But that still explains only four opinions of the nine votes in the majority. Also in the majority is Nagendra Singh, who voted for interim measures applauding the Court's "positive test regarding its own competence."[2] Singh is regularly viewed as a judge in tune with the newer interpretation of the Court's role. Because the majority opinion did not speak to the jurisdictional questions directly, it is just guesswork as to what the Court's final vote might have been on jurisdiction and the larger customary law questions.

But, even if one assumes that in this case the Court had been persuaded by the politics of the situation, the remaining caseload evidence is still impressive. In light of the number of the other cases examined herein, this would be seen as more of an aberration. It is not beyond the realm of possibility that this decision was but a temporary backlash among the Court's judges to their 1971 *Namibia* decision, in which they had made such a strong statement in the underdeveloped realm of the law of nondiscrimination—the Court showing itself as not out of control, if you will. Pronouncing in two such controversial areas of customary law within such a short period might have been viewed as too activist, and brought reproach to the Court.

It should also be noted that there are three other cases accepted by the Court that have not been included here for full analysis. There are some who might argue that the *Aegean Sea Continental Shelf* case (1978), pitting Greece against Turkey, should be included in this exploration of the cases of the ICJ. After all, in Turkey's letter of April 24, 1978, declaring that Turkey would not participate in the proceedings before the Court, the dispute was referred to as one "of a highly political nature."[3] The Court did take note of this argument, and responded that such a dispute "in respect of the delimitation of their continental shelf can hardly fail to have some political element."[4] But this was a *very* tangential line of argument on Turkey's part, not at all the main thrust of its objection to the Court's jurisdiction (the contention that the two textual sources of jurisdiction upon which Greece relied were not valid ones). The result is that I have chosen not to include extensive analysis of this case.

The same reasoning holds for *Western Sahara* (1975). The political overtones of the case were not the basis for Spain's objections to the Court's jurisdiction. And, in the advisory opinion from the World Health Organization (WHO) on the *Host Agreement* case (1980), the politics swirling around the dispute were not raised at all in the oral or written arguments before the Court. The Court took note of the suggestion made during WHO debates that the Court should not accept the case because opponents of the proposal insisted that it was nothing but a political maneuver designed to postpone any decision concerning removal of the Regional Office from Egypt. But, again, the Court denied that such concerns had any bearing on the Court's jurisdiction or response. In all three of these cases, the Court looked past the politics involved to accept jurisdiction, so not including them does not change the conclusions of the book. In fact, including them could only strengthen these conclusions.

One of these conclusions is certainly that the ICJ has shown itself to be as willing as the PCIJ to accept jurisdiction in disputes that have significant political aspects, refusing to allow the objections concerning the politics of a dispute to bar jurisdiction. Another way of saying this is that regardless of the approach taken interpretation-wise, restrictive or expansive, the Courts have never been faced with subject matter that was viewed as incapable of legal resolution.

With this conclusion in mind, now would be the time to glance back over Chapter 1, the chapter tracing scholarly opinion on this matter, and Chapter 2, the chapter tracing state practice on this matter, and remind oneself of the results of those two chapters. With but a few exceptions, the scholarly community has heavily favored the realist position, which would require that conflicts in international intercourse be divided into two categories, legal and non-legal (or political). So too with the position of states as drawn from the evidence of state practice.

However, the discerning eye will note that the actions of the PCIJ and ICJ indicate that the two courts have been more attuned to the argument that has been associated with the idealist position, that there are no *lacunae*, or gaps, in the law. It was Lauterpacht and Higgins, in 1933 and 1968 respectively, who argued that international law, like municipal law, should be viewed as a complete system of law. "The prohibition of *non liquet* is one of the general principles of law recognised by civilized nations," wrote Lauterpacht.[5] By the evidence presented here, the PCIJ and the ICJ appear to agree.

This is an extremely important difference of opinion, that between the majority of the scholarly community and the states on the one hand and the Court on the other. That is because there is a big difference between saying that the law reaches all actions within a group's intercourse or it does not. If one holds the position that the law does not reach all actions, then one has, metaphorically, opened the door a crack. And after doing that, how open the door is becomes a subjective call. A state is apt to claim that because the Court's purview did not reach dispute A that it really does not reach dispute B either, and so forth. Thus, whether the door opens enough to allow through 1 percent of international intercourse or 2 percent or 5 percent becomes open to debate. And whatever the size of that sliver of disputes not susceptible of judicial resolution, that sliver represents anarchy.

Therein lies the difference between saying all issues are justiciable and saying some are not. Lauterpacht should receive his due finally, because the PCIJ and the ICJ agree with him that there is no room in international relations for anarchical behavior. What was earlier a rejected theoretical position has now become the dominant position at the ICJ. Chapters 1 and 2 began as simple contextual chapters, but they have served an even larger role: highlighting the importance of the work of the ICJ. The Court's jurisprudence strongly favors the justiciability of all issues. This jurisprudence stands in stark contrast to those who argue that international law is weak. International law is not weak. Only the will to utilize and enforce it is.

This difference of positions also raises the need to address the definition of justiciable in international law. As was pointed out in the Introduction, *Black's Law Dictionary* equates "justiciable" with "appropriate." As has been indicated here, as long as one relied on scholars of the realist school or states to define appropriate, that definition had very little meaning. The term justiciable did not carry the same weight it does in municipal law, as a result of the subjectivity surrounding it. In the final analysis, a dispute was justiciable if the states involved agreed it was. Thus, the definition of justiciable varied from state to state and over time.

That indeterminateness no longer exists according to the evidence presented here. "Appropriate for judicial determination" no longer contains the element "absence of political context." It may be that at one time states equated "non-justiciable" with "political," but that has been shown here to be no longer a viable position. The international community must aquaint itself with a new working definition of the term justiciable.

The two Courts have taken very seriously Article 36(6) of their respective Statutes granting them the power to determine their own jurisdiction where a question over that jurisdiction arises. In doing so, they have given wide interpretation to the term "legal disputes." The PCIJ and the ICJ have shown themselves until now to be willing to apply the law to any situation, if given the chance (i.e., if a dispute is presented to them), regardless of surrounding "high politics." Is this a trend that one should expect to continue? The answer to this question may lie in the conclusions one reaches about Edward McWhinney's theory about the jurisprudence of both Courts.

McWhinney, it should be remembered, argued that whereas many times people speak of the jurisprudence of the Permanent Court of International Justice and the jurisprudence of the International Court of Justice as two separate entities, it might be more appropriate to consider them as one whole corpus. As he saw the jurisprudence of the entire seven-decade span, however, there was still a break of which to take note. For McWhinney, that break occurred in the aftermath of the 1966 *South West Africa* judgment.

But in proving his case, McWhinney set himself up for the possible line of criticism that, by using so few cases as examples, he chose *only* the right cases to prove his point. I believe I have moved on McWhinney's valuable construct in what might be a more objective manner. The cases included in Chapters 3 and 4 were not chosen by me. Rather, they simply represent that subset of the two Courts' body of work in which the legal nature of the dispute was in question. This straightforward categorization left no room for a charge of favoritism. I present this examination of these cases as an objective test of McWhinney's theory.

The result of this effort is very supportive of McWhinney. The theories of interpretation that held sway over the work of the two Courts, as seen in the cases examined herein, appear to be just as McWhinney suggested. That is, the Courts were more positivist before 1966, and more given to a teleological, or natural law, style of interpretation thereafter.

As was pointed out at the end of Chapter 3 by Fockema Andreae, the reasoning underlying the judgments of the Permanent Court of International Justice remained within a very limited view of a court's role, especially an international court. The PCIJ was careful that its role was seen clearly as interpreter of the law and no more. At that, it was the law that was either expressly written in a text, or it was the law as expressly intended by the framers of a text. Intervening history was not a factor weighed seriously by the PCIJ.

Prior to 1966, the decisions of the ICJ were also nearly bereft of references to customary law and general law. Social context and "just," outcome-based decision making were not regarded as juridical concerns. The Court's philosophy was epiphenomenological in its orientation. In other words, it felt there existed some other realm of issues outside of its own preset boundaries of finding the law. The Court viewed itself as constituted by states to settle differences of interpretation between states over the rules created by states.

Change did come. It was originally heralded as necessary by Judge Alvarez, who felt that international law was different as a result of World War II and his fellow judges just had not reached the same conclusion yet. But he found himself more often than not in the minority, having to write dissent after dissent. Judge Jessup, too, called for a wider view of the Court's role, in 1966's *South West Africa* case. What was more indicative of the time was Judges Spender and Fitzmaurice's dissent in the 1962 phase of *South West Africa*, (and would be the majority opinion in 1966), when they wrote:

> We are not unmindful of, nor are we insensible to, the various considerations of a non-juridical character, social, humanitarian and other, which underlie this case; but these are matters for the political rather that the legal arena. They cannot be allowed to deflect us from our duty of reaching a conclusion strictly on the basis of what we believe to be the correct legal view.[6]

But, again, this position's time was limited, and this may best be heard in the words of a dissenter worried over the new role of the Court. Listen to Judge Ignacio-Pinto's declaration in *Fisheries Jurisdiction*:

> In taking this viewpoint I am not unaware of the risk that I may be accused of not being in tune with the modern trend for the Court to arrogate a creative power which does not pertain to it under either the United Nations Charter or its Statute. Perhaps some might even say that the classic conception of international law to which I declare allegiance is out-dated; but for myself, I do not fear to continue to respect the classic norms of that law. Perhaps from the Third Conference on the Law of the Sea some positive principles accepted by all States will emerge. I hope this will be so, and shall be the first to applaud—and furthermore I shall be pleased to see the good use to which they can be put, in particular for the benefit of the developing countries. But since I am above all faithful to judicial practice, I continue fervently to urge the need for the Court to confine itself to its obligation to state the law as it is at present in relation to the facts of the case brought before it.[7]

Beginning with the 1971 *Namibia* decision, the Court willingly and openly discussed topics such as the higher social-benefit goals of South Africa's mandate, the equitable sharing of the resources of the seas, and the humanitarian concerns trampled by the act of hostage-taking. The ICJ was favorably inclined toward venturing off of the more straightforward (and one might argue safer) path of textual interpretation, and into that of customary law and general principles of law (what might be more equated with the shared norms of the community), in its search for the sources of international law. This philosophy was more phenomenological in its orientation—all knowledge was relevant to the administering of justice.

This epiphenomenological/phenomenological difference over what is relied upon as a source of law for dispute resolution is a very important point that requires as much emphasis as it can be given. *There is a real connection that should be seen between the sources of law the Court will reference and the role the Court sees for itself in the international arena.* Customary law and general principles of law *are* listed in the Court's Statute as valid sources of the law for the Court to utilize. But it did not utilize these sources once upon a time. Constricting itself to examining only what states had actually agreed to on paper also served to constrict the Court's *role*. That role then was the Court as a reactive body (not reactive in the sense that it must be moved to action by its client states, which still holds true for the Court in 1993, but rather, as even allowing the boundaries of applicable law to be set for it, that of the relevant texts).

By expanding what it saw as legitimate sources of the law (into the shared norms of the community), the Court has expanded its role into that of the Court as active participant. It may define what the law is. This allows it to be more normative in its analysis if it feels that the situation requires it. It may also set states on the path toward desirable future goals, something the Court would never have considered until 1966. In that regard the Court feels comfortable in taking responsibility for the future well-being of the Namibians or the sharing of the world's sea resources. The Court now feels comfortable chastising a state for disobeying the Court, as it did in *Diplomatic and Consular Staff* when it branded the United States rescue attempt as being in contradistinction to its order against inflamatory actions by *either* state, handed down in the interim measures phase of the case. To read the decisions of the Court is to move from strict interpretation to expounding on the law, from analysis to narrative.

Its role as active participant may certainly be seen in the increased direction the Court has been willing to give to the disputants before it. In *Fisheries Jurisdiction*, *Nuclear Tests*, *Diplomatic and Consular Staff*, and the *Nicaragua* cases, the Court ordered interim measures. In *Fisheries Jurisdiction*, the Court directed the disputants to negotiations. In *Nicaragua*, the Court arranged for the case to be returned to it should Nicaragua and the United States be unable to settle their differences over damages. This are just a few examples of a marked increase in interaction with the cases before it.

McWhinney was right in his construct of a positivist/post-positivist split in the Court's jurisprudence at 1966—the Court has expanded its view of its own role in the international arena. If one were to apply the terminology of American constitutional law to all that I have just written, one would say the Court has moved from judicial restraint to judicial activism. How does knowing this answer the question raised above: With the evidence presented so far, is it reasonable to assume that the International Court of Justice will continue to refuse to allow political context to bar its review of a dispute? The Court showed itself disinclined to turn away political cases when it had a narrow view of its role. There is less reason to believe it will do so now that the Court has come to view its role as that of another dispute-resolving avenue. The International Court of Justice does not see itself bound by considerations of political context, and it will not in the future. What has emerged is a more activist Court.

There is a modification of McWhinney's theory that should be made. There have been instances since 1966 where the Court has still been asked to interpet texts, and one may expect that this will always be a role the ICJ will perform. As such, it is not actually the entirety of the ICJ's caseload that supports the theory that the Court has allowed for a wider role for itself. It is only in those instances where the Court has the opportunity to reference and illuminate customary law and general principles of law that such evidence appears.

These conclusions—that the PCIJ and the ICJ have not allowed the politics of a dispute to affect their jurisdiction, that McWhinney's theory regarding a new idealist and activist mindset at the Court is correct, that the ICJ is likely to continue not recognizing a political question bar to its jurisdiction, and that this results in the reformulation of the definition of justiciable in international law—lead in a very definite direction, which is back to the Introduction. It was there that finding out if a political question doctrine existed in international law was listed as a chief goal of this book. It was there that I noted that some thought that finding a division between law and politics is impossible to do. This examination indicates that such a debate is merely an academic exercise. With the possible exception of *Nuclear Tests*, neither Court has turned down any case, no matter how heavy with politics the dispute may have been. While scholars have been arguing back and forth over what disputes are capable of legal resolution, the Courts themselves have been quietly, and maybe even unnoticed if the continuation of the scholarly debate is any indication, establishing their own jurisprudence on the subject.

It could be suggested that such a conclusion will have a deliterious effect on state actions regarding the Court. What of the possibility of the Court being viewed as too freewheeling to be trusted with dispute resolution? What of the possibility of states being afraid to accept the Court's compulsory jurisdiction under such conditions, and thus declining the opportunity to do so? I have several answers to this concern.

As it stands, the International Court of Justice's docket has never been busier. There are quite a number of cases currently before the Court. The disputants in these cases have not raised any objections as to the political nature, or the vital interest, of their respective disputes. This should be seen as some evidence that states are increasingly viewing the Court as an alternative avenue of dispute resolution, which tends to show that states are not afraid of international adjudication. The logjam is breaking up, as it were. One possible outcome of this busy schedule is that as the Court resolves more disputes, states should continue to become more relaxed about international adjudication, and more confident in it, and concerns over the possibility of the Court trampling sovereign rights will fade.

It is also the case that the number of acceptances of the compulsory jurisdiction of the Court has steadily increased over the last several years. When the United States dropped its acceptance of the Court's compulsory jurisdiction, the number of acceptances dropped to 45, and there was some concern that the U.S. example might lead others to do the same. In fact, just the opposite has occurred. The number of acceptances has now risen to 54. This also suggests greater respect and trust for the Court.

In the final analysis, though, it is not the Court's problem to deal with, anyhow. There are those who caution that states should be cautious of the cases they take to the Court, excising any with political overtones, so as to not put the Court in the uncomfortable position of having to worry over non-compliance making it look ineffective. But that is just blame-shifting—the Court is not ineffective, as we have seen. It can find "the law." If states do not follow up, that is not the Court's fault, and the Court has noted on several occasions that it cannot be deterred from its mission by the prospect of non-compliance. Blame for any perceived inadequacies in international adjudication should be placed at the feet of states and no excuses should be made for them or cautions given to the Court in its acceptance of cases.

After all, whose reputation was tarnished and whose was enhanced by the *Namibia* decision? By the *Nicaragua* decision? It was the non-complying South Africa and the non-complying United States who had black eyes before the court of world opinion. In both decisions, it was the Court that had its reputation burnished. It may even be that these decisions proved to some the independence of the Court, and helped lead to the increased use of the Court noted above. The point is that the Court cannot, and should not, change its jurisprudence or tinker with its Statute in order to differentiate between legal and political questions just to suit the fears of some states. The Court must continue to reach its decisions unimpaired by the prospects of state reaction. To act otherwise would serve to make it appear willing to be bent by the will of its clients and thus less like a court of law. In the end, it is only by being independent of the will of its clients that it can maintain its strength as an institution of dispute resolution.

The greatest initial objection I anticipate to my conclusions is that they are not a realistic assessment of state practice. That is true. State practice more closely resembles the old positions of John Westlake or Thomas Willing Balch. In other words, states are very positivist and very protective of state sovereignty.

States have not made significant use of the International Court of Justice over the years. States have not signed on to compulsory jurisdiction in droves. Occasionally, states have outright defied the decisions of the Court. Worse yet, as Scott and Csajko[8] clearly show, the Court has actually been used on occasion to satisfy states' own political agendas. Scott and Csajko list the United States' many submissions against Warsaw Pact states in the 1950s, the *Diplomatic and Consular Staff* case, and the *Nicaragua* case as just such uses of the Court.

On the other hand, this *is* a realistic assessment of the jurisprudence of the Permanent Court of International Justice and the International Court of Justice. These two international adjudicative bodies have shown themselves no more willing to be swayed by the fears of disputants that their freedom of movement will be constricted, than is any national adjudicative body. It may seem ironic, but it is nonetheless true, that while international law is state-consent driven, the possible loss of some measure of sovereign rights is not a legal argument sustainable in court. A claim that vital interests are at stake is an attempt to cordon off certain subject matter as too closely tied to sovereignty to allow third-party intervention. As has been shown, the two Courts have not recognized such an objection to jurisdiction.

There appears almost an unbridgable chasm between these two positions. For me to suggest, in some normative fashion, that the Court should continue on the same course in spite of state opinion may strike some as an idealistic flight of fancy. Is this so? Maybe not.

Certainly, as has already been pointed out, the ICJ has never been busier. This suggests a possible reevaluation of the ICJ. This seemingly coincides with a broader reevaluation of the usefulness of supranational institutions in general. The United Nations as a whole has never been busier. A growing number of actions have been taken worldwide in the last few years under its auspices, from the Gulf War of 1990–91 to the Somalian relief effort of 1992, to the deployment of peacekeeping forces in Mozambique.

One change in the historical context in which the U.N. operates has already been alluded to as an explanation for this increase in utilization. That would be the ending of the cold war between the United States and the former Soviet Union. Throughout the years of bipolar competition, the United Nations was one site of constant confrontation between two of the powers with a veto power over Security Council activities. Action by the United Nations was regularly stymied. With the end of this superpower competition, the United Nations has much greater freedom of movement than it ever did previously.

Another possible explanation for this might follow along the lines of Gerald Rabow's suggestions, for mechanisms of peaceful dispute resolution.[9] His prescriptions flowed from the field of game theory. Cooperation makes sense because it serves the disputants' interests best. Rabow worried over the threat of a nuclear exchange. But it may be that in today's economic climate, states are more worried over the financial cost of disputes. The old transnationalist arguments of interdependence may finally hit home, what with the disruption of trade, the displacement of people (meaning the possible absorbsion of refugees), and other side effects of disputes. Additionally, states may wish to spread around the cost of dispute resolution.

These may not be noble reasons for renewed interest in international mechanisms of dispute resolution, but who is to argue with the endpoint. The point is that states appear to be inching their way toward relinquishing bits and pieces of sovereignty for the commonweal. The Court's docket may indicate that this trend is having a coattails effect for the Court.

The Secretary General of the United Nations has added his own voice to creating an impression that now is a new era for peaceful dispute resolution. In a report entitled "An Agenda for Peace" released on June 17, 1992, the Secretary General recommended the following optimistic step for reinforcing the role of the ICJ: "All Member States should accept the general jurisdiction of the International Court under Article 36 of its Statute, *without any reservation*, before the end of the United Nations Decade of International Law in the year 2000."[10]

Beyond that, anyone familiar with the decisions of the Court will recognize just how thorough the Court has been in satisfying itself that it does have jurisdiction. Rather than fear the power of the Court to settle disputes as to its jurisdiction, states should appeciate the great care taken by the Court in undertaking its casework. Such care does not speak of an institution eager to flex its muscles at every opportunity and plow under the rights of states. Instead, it bespeaks an institution that has earned trust.

I undertook to examine the hypothetical existence of a distinction between legal and political questions in international law, or more precisely, before international tribunals. I have found that, by their actions, the Permanent Court of International Justice and International Court of Justice have built a jurisprudence that does not admit of such a distinction. It is to be acknowledged that states could draw away from the Court on the basis of this news. It is to be hoped that they will not. The choice is inevitably theirs to make. International adjudication has proven itself worthy. With a little luck, states will act accordingly.

Notes

INTRODUCTION

1. U.S. Department of State 1985.
2. Brownlie 1967, 123.
3. McWhinney 1990, 45.

CHAPTER 1

1. Vattel [1916] 1964, 224.
2. Vattel [1916] 1964, 225.
3. Oppenheim [1952-55] 1967, 3-4.
4. Westlake 1910, 358.
5. Balch [1874] 1915, 12.
6. Balch [1874] 1915, 35.
7. Balch [1874] 1915, 37.
8. Balch [1874] 1915, 37.
9. Balch 1924, 6-7.
10. Borchard 1924, 53.
11. Borchard 1924, 55-56.
12. Hudson 1924, 127.
13. Lauterpacht [1933] 1966, 3.
14. Lauterpacht [1933] 1966, 64.
15. Lauterpacht [1933] 1966, 64.
16. Lauterpacht [1933] 1966, 153.
17. Lauterpacht [1933] 1966, 249.
18. Lauterpacht [1933] 1966, 255.

19. Lauterpacht [1933] 1966, 351.
20. Kelsen 1966.
21. Kelsen 1966.
22. Kelsen 1944, 24.
23. Kelsen 1966, 526.
24. Morgenthau [1948] 1973, 435.
25. Lissitzyn 1972, 71.
26. Norton 1987, 499.
27. Falk 1971.
28. Bickel 1962.
29. Rogoff 1989, 299.
30. Wani 1986, 469.
31. Lissitzyn 1972, 74.
32. Mosler 1988.
33. Anand 1974, 233.
34. Anand 1974, 241.
35. Higgins 1968, 60.
36. Higgins 1968, 74.
37. Higgins 1968, 83.
38. Clark and Sohn 1966.
39. Henkin 1968.

CHAPTER 2

1. Ralston 1929, 157.
2. Ralston 1929.
3. Balch [1874] 1915, 6.
4. Balch [1874] 1915.
5. Scott 1916, 207-8.
6. Scott 1931, 40.
7. Cory 1932, 10.
8. Scott 1917, 3.
9. Scott 1917, 95.
10. Brown 1925, 270.
11. Hudson [1943] 1972.
12. Scott 1917, 35.
13. Hudson 1944.
14. Lauterpacht [1933] 1966, 30.
15. Lauterpacht [1933] 1966.
16. Cory 1932.

17. For a list of those registered with the Secretariat of the League of Nations (which the Secretariat felt was all but a very few of these type), see bibliography under League of Nations 1926.
18. Habicht 1931, 285.
19. Habicht 1931, 680.
20. Oppenheim [1952-55] 1967, 31-32.
21. Habicht 1931, 638.
22. Habicht 1931, 75-76.
23. League of Nations 1926.
24. United Nations 1949, 3.
25. Sohn 1990.
26. UN Document A/CN.4/113, March 6, 1958.
27. Oellers-Frahm and Wuhler 1984; Sohn 1990.
28. Sohn 1990.
29. Brownlie 1990; Koojimans 1990; Lachs 1990.

CHAPTER 3

1. Anand 1974; Cory 1932.
2. Hudson [1943] 1972; Bledsoe and Boczek 1987.
3. Hudson [1943] 1972, 412.
4. Hudson 1944, 72.
5. PCIJ Series B, No. 16, p. 20.
6. PCIJ Series B, No. 4, pp. 18-19.
7. PCIJ Series B, No. 4, p. 23.
8. PCIJ Series B, No. 4, p. 21.
9. PCIJ Series B, No. 4, p. 24.
10. PCIJ Series B, No. 4, p. 24.
11. PCIJ Series B, No. 4, p. 25.
12. PCIJ Series B, No. 4, p. 25.
13. PCIJ Series B, No. 5, p. 12.
14. PCIJ Series B, No. 5, p. 27.
15. PCIJ Series B, No. 12, p. 19.
16. PCIJ Series B, No. 12, p. 11.
17. PCIJ Series B, No. 12, p. 6.
18. PCIJ Series B, No. 12, p. 8.
19. PCIJ Series B, No. 12, p. 26.
20. PCIJ Series B, No. 12, p. 27.
21. PCIJ Series B, No. 12, p. 27.
22. PCIJ Series B, No. 13, pp. 9-10.
23. PCIJ Series B, No. 13, p. 14.
24. PCIJ Series B, No. 13, pp. 21-23.

25. PCIJ Series A, No. 15, p. 10.
26. PCIJ Series A, No. 15, p. 24.
27. PCIJ Series A, No. 15, p. 22.
28. PCIJ Series A, Nos. 20/21, pp. 19-20.
29. PCIJ Series A/B, Fascicule No. 46, p. 128.
30. PCIJ Series A, No. 22, p. 7.
31. PCIJ Series A/B, Fascicule No. 46, p. 153.
32. PCIJ Series A/B, Fascicule No. 46, p. 162.
33. PCIJ Series A/B, Fascicule No. 41, p. 42.
34. PCIJ Series A/B, Fascicule No. 41, p. 43.
35. Hudson 1938, 210.
36. PCIJ Series A/B, Fascicule No. 41, p. 42.
37. PCIJ Series A/B, Fascicule No. 41, p. 70.
38. PCIJ Series A/B, Fascicule No. 41, p. 75.
39. PCIJ Series A/B, Fascicule No. 41, pp. 75-76.
40. PCIJ Series A/B, Fascicule No. 41, p. 68.
41. Fockema Andreae 1948, 134.
42. Fockema Andreae 1948, 134.
43. Falk 1986, 176.

CHAPTER 4

1. Lissitzyn [1951] 1972, 53.
2. Rosenne 1957.
3. McWhinney 1990, xvii.
4. McWhinney 1990, 21.
5. Von Glahn 1981.
6. McWhinney 1990.
7. McWhinney 1990, xvii.
8. ICJ Reports 1948, 70.
9. ICJ Reports 1948, 58.
10. ICJ Reports 1948, 61.
11. ICJ Reports 1948, 77.
12. ICJ Reports 1948, 75.
13. ICJ Reports 1948, 95.
14. Lissitzyn [1951] 1972, 91.
15. ICJ Reports 1950, 5.
16. ICJ Reports 1950, 288.
17. ICJ Reports 1950, 402.
18. ICJ Reports 1950, 79.
19. ICJ Reports 1960, 53.
20. Riggs and Plano 188.

21. Lefever 1967, 202.
22. Lefever 1967, 200.
23. ICJ Reports 1962, 155.
24. ICJ Reports 1962, 344.
25. ICJ Reports 1966, 18.
26. ICJ Reports 1966, 21.
27. ICJ Reports 1966, 22.
28. Rosenne 1989.
29. ICJ Reports 1971, 39.
30. ICJ Reports 1971, 17.
31. ICJ Reports 1971, 31.
32. ICJ Reports 1971, 31-2.
33. ICJ Reports 1974, 10.
34. ICJ Reports 1973, 20.
35. ICJ Reports 1974, 37.
36. Rosenne 1989.
37. ICJ Reports 1974, 31.
38. ICJ Reports 1973, 100.
39. ICJ Reports 1973, 102.
40. ICJ Reports 1973, 106.
41. ICJ Reports 1973, 133.
42. ICJ Reports 1973, 126.
43. ICJ Reports 1980, 8-9.
44. ICJ Reports 1980, 20.
45. ICJ Reports 1983-84, 398.
46. ICJ Reports 1983-84, 436.
47. ICJ Reports 1983-84, 429.
48. ICJ Reports 1983-84, 434.
49. ICJ Reports 1986, 17.
50. U.S. Dept. of State 1985.
51. ICJ Reports 1983-84, 434.
52. ICJ Reports 1983-84, 434.
53. ICJ Reports 1988, 73.
54. ICJ Reports 1988, 91.
55. ICJ Reports 1988, 91.

CHAPTER 5

1. Dugard 1976, 483.
2. ICJ Reports 1974, 108.
3. ICJ Reports 1978, 13.
4. ICJ Reports 1978, 13.

5.   Lauterpacht 1933 [1966], 67.
6.   ICJ Reports 1962, 466.
7.   ICJ Reports 1974, 37-8.
8.   Scott and Csajko 1988.
9.   Rabow 1990.
10. (emphasis added) U.N. A/47/277 1992, 965.

Bibliography

Anand, Ram Prakash. 1974. *International Courts and Contemporary Conflicts.* New York: Asia Publishing House.

Balch, Thomas [1874] 1915. *International Courts of Arbitration.* Thomas Willing Balch, ed. Philadelphia: Allen, Lane and Scott.

Balch, Thomas Willing. 1924. *Legal and Political Questions Between Nations.* Philadelphia: Allen, Lane and Scott.

Bickel, Alexander M. 1962. *The Least Dangerous Branch.* Indianapolis: Bobbs-Merrill.

Bledsoe, Robert L. and Boleslaw A. Boczek. 1987. *The International Law Dictionary.* Santa Barbara, CA: ABC-Clio.

Bloomfield, Lincoln. 1958. "Law, Politics and International Disputes." *International Conciliation* 516:267.

Borchard, Edwin M. 1924. "The Distinction Between Legal and Political Questions." *American Society of International Law Proceedings* 18:50.

_____. 1943. "The Place of Law and Courts in International Relations." *American Journal of International Law* 37:46.

Brown, Philip Marshall. 1925. "The Classification of International Disputes." *University of Pennsylvania Law Review* 73:269.

Brownlie, Ian. 1967. "The Justiciability of Disputes and Issues in International Relations." *British Yearbook of International Law* 42:123.

_____. 1990. "Arbitration and International Adjudication," in A.H.A. Soons, *International Arbitration: Past and Prospects.* Dordrecht: Martinus Nijhoff.

Clark, Grenville, and Louis B. Sohn. 1966. *World Peace Through World Law.* Cambridge: Harvard University Press.

Cory, Helen May. 1932. *Compulsory Arbitration of International Disputes.* New York: Columbia University Press.

David Davies Memorial Institute of International Studies. 1972. *International Disputes: The Legal Aspects*. London: Europa Publications.

Dugard, John. 1976. "The Nuclear Tests Cases and the South West Africa Cases: Some Realism About the Judicial Decision." *Virginia Journal of International Law* 16:463.

Falk, Richard. 1971. "Realistic Horizons for International Adjudication." *Virginia Journal of International Law* 11:314.

_____. 1986. *Reviving the World Court*. Princeton, N.J.: Princeton University Press.

Farachi, Alexander P. 1925. *The Permanent Court of International Justice: Its Constitution, Procedure and Work*. London: Oxford University Press.

Fockema Andreae, J. P. 1948. *An Important Chapter From The History of Legal Interpretation*. Leyden, The Netherlands: A. W. Sijthoff.

Fox, Hazel. 1988. "States and the Undertaking to Arbitrate." *International and Comparative Law Quarterly* 37:1.

Gilmore, Grant. 1946. "The International Court of Justice." *Yale Law Journal* 55:1049.

Giustini, Anthony. 1986. "Compulsory Adjudication in International Law: The Past, the Present, and Prospects for the Future." *Fordham International Law Journal* 9:213–56.

Grieves, Forest L. 1969. *Supranationalism and International Adjudication*. Urbana: University of Illinois Press.

Habicht, Max. 1931. *Post-War Treaties for the Pacific Settlement of International Disputes*. Cambridge: Harvard University Press.

Henkin, Louis. 1968. *How Nations Behave*. New York: Praeger.

Higgins, Rosalyn. 1968. "Policy Considerations and the International Judicial Process." *International and Comparative Law Quarterly* 17:58.

Hubbard, Heidi K. 1985. "Separation of Powers Within the United Nations: A Revised Role for the International Court of Justice." *Stanford Law Review* 38:163.

Hudson, Manley O. 1924. "Legal and Political Questions." *American Society of International Law Proceedings* 18:126.

_____. 1931. *The World Court: 1921–1931*. Boston: World Peace Foundation.

_____, ed. [1934–43] 1969. *World Court Reports*. Dobbs Ferry, N.Y.: Oceana Publications.

_____. [1943] 1972. *The Permanent Court of International Justice, 1920–1942*. Reprint. New York: Arno Press.

_____. 1944. *International Tribunals: Past and Future*. Washington, D.C.: Carnegie Endowment for International Peace and Brookings Institution.

International Court of Justice. *Reports of Judgements, Advisory Opinions and Orders*. Leyden, The Netherlands: A. W. Sijthoff.

Jenks, C. Wilfred. 1950. *The World Beyond the Charter*. London: George Allen and Unwin.

Jully, Laurent. 1954. "Arbitration and Judicial Settlement—Recent Trends." *American Journal of International Law* 48:380.

Kelsen, Hans. 1940. "Essential Conditions of International Justice." *American Society of International Law Proceedings* 35:70.

_____. 1943. "Compulsory Adjudication of International Disputes." *American Journal of International Law* 37:397.

_____. 1944. *Peace Through Law*. Chapel Hill: University of North Carolina Press.

_____. 1950. *The Law of the United Nations*. New York: Frederick A. Praeger.

_____. 1966. *Principles of International Law*. Robert W. Tucker, ed. New York: Holt, Rinehart and Winston.

Koojimans, P. H. 1990. "International Arbitration in Historical Perspective: Past and Present," in A.H.A. Soons, *International Arbitration: Past and Prospects*. Dordrecht: Martinus Nijhoff.

La Calamita, John. 1985. "The 'World Court': Coping with Political Realism and the Sovereign Tribe in International Adjudication." *Ottawa Law Review* 17:553.

Lachs, M. 1990. "Arbitration and International Adjudication," in A.H.A. Soons, *International Arbitration: Past and Prospects*. Dordrecht: Martinus Nijhoff.

Lauterpacht, Hersch. [1933] 1966. *The Function of Law in the International Community*. Reprint. Hamden, Conn.: Archon Books.

League of Nations. 1926. *Arbitration and Security: Systematic Survey of The Arbitration Conventions and Treaties of Mutual Security Deposited with The League of Nations*. Publications of the League of Nations.

Lefever, Ernest W. 1967. *Uncertain Mandate: Politics of the U.N. Congo Operation*. Baltimore: Johns Hopkins University Press.

Lissitzyn, Oliver J. [1951] 1972. *The International Court of Justice*. New York: Octagon Books.

McWhinney, Edward. 1990. *Judicial Settlement of International Disputes*. Dordrecht: Martinus Nijhoff.

Merrills, J.G. 1969. "The Justiciability of International Disputes." *Canada Bar Review* 47:241.

Morgenthau, Hans. [1948] 1973. *Politics Among Nations*. Reprint. New York: Alfred A. Knopf.

_____. 1974. "International Law and International Politics: An Uneasy Partnership." *American Society of International Law Proceedings* 68:331.

Mosler, Hermann. 1988. "Political and Justiciable Legal Disputes: Revival of an Old Controversy?" in Bin Cheng and E. D. Brown, eds. *Contemporary Problems of International Law*. London: Stevens and Sons.

Northedge, F. S., and M. D. Donelan. 1971. *International Disputes: The Political Aspects*. London: Europa Publications.

Norton, Patrick M. 1987. "The *Nicaragua* Case: Political Questions Before the International Court of Justice." *Virginia Journal of International Law* 23:459–526.

Oellers-Frahm, Karin, and Norbert Wuhler. 1984. *Dispute Settlement in Public International Law*. Berlin: Springer Verlag.

Oppenheim, Lassa. [1952–1955] 1967. *International Law*. 2 vols., Hersch Lauterpacht, ed. New York: David McKay.

Permanent Court of International Justice. *Reports: Series A, Series B, Series A/B*. Leyden, The Netherlands: A. W. Sijthoff.

Rabow, Gerald. 1990. *Peace Through Agreement*. New York: Praeger.

Ralston, Jackson. 1929. *International Arbitration from Athens to Locarno*. Stanford: Stanford University Press.

Riggs, Robert E., and Jack C. Plano. 1988. *The United Nations*, Chicago: Dorsey Press.

Rogoff, Martin A. 1989. "International Politics and the Rule of Law: The United States and the International Court of Justice." *Boston University International Law Journal* 7:272.

Rosenne, Shabtai. 1957. *The International Court of Justice*. Leyden, The Netherlands: A. W. Sijthoff.

_____. 1965. *The Law and Practice of the International Court of Justice*. Leyden, The Netherlands: A. W. Sijthoff.

_____. 1989. *The World Court: What It Is and How It Works*. Dordrecht, The Netherlands: Martinus Nijhoff.

Scott, Gary L., and Karen D. Csajko. 1988. "Compulsory Jurisdiction and Defiance in the World Court: A Comparison of the PCIJ and the ICJ." *Denver Journal of International Law and Policy* 16(2,3):377–92.

Scott, James Brown, ed. 1916. *Resolutions of the Institute of International Law*. New York: Oxford University Press.

_____, ed. 1917. *Reports to the Hague Conferences of 1899 and 1907*. Oxford: Clarendon Press.

_____. 1931. *International Conferences of American States*. New York: Oxford University Press.

Simpson, J. L., and Hazel Fox. 1959. *International Arbitration*. New York: Frederick A. Praeger.

Singh, Nagendra. 1989. *The Role and Record of the International Court of Justice*. Dordrecht: Martinus Nijhoff.

Sohn, Louis B. 1944. "Exclusion of Political Disputes from Judicial Settlement." *American Journal of International Law* 38:694.

_____. 1983. "The Role of Arbitration in Recent International Multilateral Treaties." *Virginia Journal of International Law* 23:171.

_____. 1990. "International Arbitration in Historical Perspective: Past and Present," in A.H.A. Soons, *International Arbitration: Past and Prospects*. Dordrecht: Martinus Nijhoff.

Steinberger, Helmut. 1982. "Judicial Settlement of International Disputes," in R. Bernhardt, ed., *Encyclopedia of Public International Law*, 2:120. Amsterdam: North-Holland. 1981–90.

Stone, Julius. 1959. *Legal Controls of International Conflict*. New York: Rinehart.

Stuyt, A. M. 1972. *Survey of International Arbitrations: 1794–1970*. Leyden, The Netherlands: A. W. Sijthoff.

United Nations. 1949. *Systematic Survey of Treaties for the Pacific Settlement of International Disputes: 1928–48*. Lake Success, N.Y.: United Nations Publications.

_____. 1966. *A Survey of Treaty Provisions for the Pacific Settlement of International Disputes: 1949–62*. New York: United Nations Publications.

_____. (Annual Series). *Reports of International Arbitral Awards*. New York: United Nations Publications.

_____. (Annual Series). *Yearbook of the United Nations*. New York: Office of Public Information, United Nations.

United States Department of State. 1985. "U.S. Withdrawal from the Proceedings Initiated by Nicaragua in the International Court of Justice." *Department of State Bulletin No. 2096.*: March.

Vattel, Emmerich de. 1916 (reprinted, 1964). *Law of Nations or, Principles of Natural Law Applied to the Conduct and Affairs of Nations and of Sovereigns*. Charles Fenwick, trans., in *The Classics of International Law* series, James Brown Scott, ed. Dobbs Ferry, N.Y.: Oceana Publications.

Von Glahn, Gerhard. 1981. *Law Among Nations*. New York: MacMillan.

Wani, Ibrahim J. 1986. "The Future of Compulsory Jurisdiction: Rethinking the Political Question Doctrine After Iran and Nicaragua." *American Society of International Law Proceedings* Annual Meeting: 468–69.

Westlake, John. 1910. *International Law*. Cambridge: The University Press.

Whiteman, Marjorie M. 1963–1973. *Digest of International Law*. Washington, D.C.: GPO.

Index

About the Author

THOMAS J. BODIE is an international relations specialist and writer residing in Pennsylvania. He received his Ph.D. in government and politics at the University of Maryland, College Park.

ISBN 0-275-95014-X

90000>

EAN

9 780275 950149

HARDCOVER BAR CODE